DATE DUE

DE 15 04			

DEMCO 38-296

STEPPING-STONES

| VOLUME 53 | MAY 1996 | PAGES 1–224 |

Stepping-Stones

The Reminiscences of a Woman Geologist in the Twentieth Century

by
KATHARINE FOWLER-BILLINGS

TRANSACTIONS

THE CONNECTICUT ACADEMY OF ARTS AND SCIENCES
POST OFFICE BOX 208211
NEW HAVEN, CONNECTICUT 06520-8211
U.S.A.

This book was composed in ITC New Baskerville, an electronic typeface based on the English Transitional typeface designed by John Baskerville during the mid-1770s.

Susan Pasternack, Editor
Composed by Elizabeth Knox, Cambridge, Massachusetts.
Printed and bound by Thomson-Shore, Inc., Dexter, Michigan.

The paper used in this publication meets the minimum requirements of American National Standard for Information Sciences—Permanence of Paper for Printed Library Materials ANSI Z39.48-1984

ISBN 1-878508-11-3

LC 96-083507

Publications of the Connecticut Academy of Arts and Sciences can be obtained directly from the Academy, P.O. Box 208211, New Haven, Connecticut 06520-8211.

To Carol the Curious

Photograph by George Billings

Kay with Carol Frost, Wellesley, 1992

Contents

ILLUSTRATIONS

I was first introduced to the geologic work of Kay Fowler-Billings when I was studying earth sciences at Dartmouth College in the 1970s. In the course of familiarizing myself with New England geology I came across her study of the Cardigan Quadrangle, published in the *Geological Society of America Bulletin* in 1937. She provided a concise description of the New Hampshire magma series and its country rocks, which we visited on class field trips. I tucked a copy of her paper into my file of geologic literature.

I thought no more of the name Katharine Fowler for ten years while I pursued my Ph.D. at the University of Cambridge. In 1983 I took a faculty position at the University of Wyoming in Laramie and became interested in studying the Laramie Anorthosite Complex, located just east of town in the Laramie Mountains. Who should have written the first description of the complex but Katharine Stevens Fowler! It seemed incredible that I should come across this woman geologist's work again, this time in the Rocky Mountains. My curiosity was aroused. Just who was this impressive person?

Her entry in *Geologists and History of Geology* introduced more mystery: her bibliographical listing included an autobiography describing her geological prospecting in Sierra Leone. I obtained a copy of the book and read it cover to cover, a fascinating account of her expeditions in which she discovered and described hematite, molybdenum, and gold deposits in the wilds of West Africa. I had done fieldwork on my own in northern Pakistan, but I doubted I could have dealt with hostile tribal chiefs and mutiny amongst native porters as she had!

What else had this remarkable woman done? Her *Who's Who of American Women* entry reported that she had married the internationally respected geologist Marland Billings, and that they had two children. She seemed to be the model of the 1980s woman who did it all — career, marriage, children — only she had been fifty years ahead of the times. I had to find out more. I picked up the telephone and called her. I can only imagine the shock it must have been to Kay to hear some strange voice on the line asking her a stream of rather personal questions: How did she get interested in geology? What did her parents think of her unconventional career? How did she manage to continue her geologic mapping projects after she was married and had children? She replied that the only way she could respond to all my questions would be by writing another book — and four months later her manuscript was in my hands.

Katharine Stevens Fowler-Billings has made lasting contributions to the geologic community with her astute field observations and geologic maps of the Laramie Mountains (Wyoming), parts of Sierra Leone (West Africa), and New Hampshire. Her publications remain standard reference works, widely available in libraries. Many of her maps are still in print. Modern petrologic and geochemical analysis depends heavily for its correct interpretation on sound field mapping, mapping that Kay Fowler-Billings has provided to subsequent generations of geologists.

I am personally indebted to Kay for her fundamental geologic work on the Laramie Anorthosite Complex, which formed the basis for my research into the petrogenesis of this rather unusual assemblage of rock types. I am also grateful to her for providing a positive, yet realistic role model of a professional woman. She embodies the enthusiastic spirit of adventure. She has the important ability to adapt to changing situations, a capacity that is especially important to women, whose roles typically change several times during their lives. Her decision to explore Sierra Leone when she was unable to accompany her husband to the Gold Coast is an example of this adaptability. Finally, she is a model of practicality. Her life story shows that with every decision that is made, others are to some degree precluded, though this is part of life that no ambitious, able person is eager to accept. Women with young families cannot be 24-hour-a-day professional geologists. Kay's response was to be a full-time geologist in the summer and a part-time one during the school year. A person with many talents, such as she, cannot pursue all to their fullest at the same time. She took geology, mothering, and conservation work in turns. Those of us who grew up in a time when we came to expect we could "do it all" can learn a lot from Katharine Fowler-Billings.

Thank you, Kay, for sharing your life with a curious stranger from Wyoming.

Carol D. Frost
University of Wyoming

I am dedicating this book of my life as a woman geologist to a voice, Carol of Wyoming, who telephoned one day to ask about my mapping work in the Laramie Mountains. What was it like in those days? Was it a difficult adjustment to go from life as an independent geologist to marriage and motherhood? And what about prospecting for gold in Africa, she wanted to know.

To answer these questions I was jolted into action. I had long played with the idea of writing a book about my life, but I was lazy. And now I am ninety years old! You were the catalyst, Carol, in bringing me down to earth. Quickly. I got out my pen as the memories crowded in.

These chapters are also dedicated to all women who take up careers and to all who read these words, men and women, who wonder about a career woman in the twentieth century.

My life is the story of a woman's struggle to establish her place in a man's world. In the recounting of my career as a geologist, you will follow me from my carefree childhood through my college days to my professional work. My first marriage in England; prospecting for gold in West Africa. My return to America; geological mapping in New Hampshire. Teaching and raising a family. A forest fire in Glacier Park; a banquet in the Kremlin. Decisions to make; a life of travel and adventure.

It was in the depths of a copper mine in Butte, Montana, that I was first acknowledged as a "real" geologist. My Irish guide, correcting the misapprehension of a miner below, called down, "This ain't no young fella. This is a 'laidy' geologist."

It has been a full life, spanning the twentieth century and circling the globe.

ACKNOWLEDGMENTS

I wish to thank Dr. Carol Frost of the University of Wyoming for inspiring me to write the story of my life as an answer to her many questions about my career. She has been helpful in so many ways.

I am grateful to Karen Melican for her computer skills and dedication in editing and putting my manuscript together. Thanks, also, to Rachel Billings for her editorial assistance. She read the text to me as she edited and made many suggestions that evoked a flood of memories. Pamela Henrikson also lent her support.

My son, George Billings, has taken much time and care in reproducing old photographs, making prints from my many albums to enhance the text. His daughter, Heather, worked on some of my African photographs. Most of the photos are my own, with the exception of those taken in Russia, which were sent to me by friends who knew my camera had "disappeared."

Since my book *The Gold Missus* (W.W. Norton, 1938, Katharine Fowler-Lunn) was long out of print, and because my three years in Sierra Leone were the most challenging of my life, I have included an abbreviated account of that period. Some of the material has been taken from *The Gold Missus*. I have once again used fictitious names to protect the people I met.

Thanks to Allen Gessen for piecing together the "jigsaw puzzle" of my story on his computer. He had to cope with my increasingly shaky writing.

I am especially grateful to Virginia Watkin, president of the Society of Women Geographers, for her interest in getting my autobiography published. And to Birgit Faber Morse, a New York member, who brought it to the attention of Catherine Skinner, chair of the publications committee of the Connecticut Academy of Arts and Sciences. Ms. Skinner had long been interested in women geologists and their struggle to find a place in what had previously been a man's field. She grasped the opportunity to have my life as a woman geologist presented as a documentary of the twentieth century.

To Susan Pasternack I give thanks for her editing of the text, and to Elizabeth Knox, who put it all together to make, I hope, a book that is of credit to the Connecticut Academy.

STEPPING-STONES

PART I

From ABC to Ph.D.

Kay with Father at Gramma's North Andover home, 1904

Carefree Childhood

I WAS BORN with the sound of the waves and the smell of the sea at our summer home in Little Boar's Head on the New Hampshire coast. To the north lay a rocky beach with a wave-cut cliff at the head, and on the south was situated a sandy beach, rimmed by low sand dunes at the edge of a salt marsh.

When Mother's pains began at three in the morning on the twelfth of June, 1902, Auntie, my father's sister, rushed up the street to the hotel to phone the doctor. She found all the doors locked. Spying a ladder, she rested it against the porch roof, climbed into an open window, located the telephone downstairs, and called for help. The doctor arrived a couple of hours later by horse and buggy to bring me into the world. This was nearly a century ago.

My early summers were spent at the seashore, swimming in the cold waters of the Atlantic, digging in the sand in the mornings and going to Rocky Beach afternoons. I liked to climb the large glacial erratics and learned to keep my balance on the shore rocks. I watched the tides come and go and collected seashells and interesting pebbles. Later, my father brought me books to identify my finds. My schoolteachers encouraged my summertime pursuits and in the fall I took great pride in exhibiting my troves of seaweed, flowers, and rocks.

One of the first things I remember was the birth of my younger brother, early in June of 1906. Informed one day that the stork was going to bring a baby to our house, I was banished from my bedroom to the guest room. Since I already had an older brother, it was a sister I wished for. To appease me, the bassinet I used for my dolls was decorated with pink flounces. Finally the night came when I was summoned to see the new arrival. When told it was a baby brother, I burst into tears.

A governess had been hired to care for the baby and to teach French to my older brother and me. She spoke French to us all the time; I don't think she knew any English. Before long we were proficient. Mademoiselle used to take us on walks in the woods, where she caught harmless garter snakes, which she killed and then skinned. She later took the skins back to France to show her friends the terrible poisonous snakes we had in the wilds of America. Mademoiselle instilled in me a lifelong fear and distrust of these reptiles.

At the shore Father ran the small ecumenical chapel that had been built by his father for Sunday worship in the community. A different minister came each summer weekend. We children were allowed to help Father count the money from the contribution box, the proceeds of which were to pay the preacher and provide funds for the upkeep of the chapel. Father always gave the minister a twenty-dollar gold piece in payment for services.

The visiting clergy were entertained for the weekend by the parishioners. One or two stayed with us during the summer. The one I remember best was Edward Everett Hale, a large, friendly man with flowing whiskers. He was the only one whose arms were long enough to completely surround (with fingers overlapping) the large oak tree behind our house. While I sat on his knee he told stories and called me "his little friend." Today, his bronze statue stands at the edge of the Boston Public Garden, where children still sit at his feet. His story, "The Man Without a Country," became a classic. I must be one of the few who remember him.

Our summer home had originally been the site of a small resort, with four rental cottages for people who came to summer at the seashore. Some of the visitors drove by carriage all the way from Philadelphia. After one of the cottages burned, Father bought the property. This was in 1899, when he married my mother. We lived in one of the houses and rented the rest.

Each June mother prepared the cottages for the arrivals. We dusted and cleaned. The lace curtains were washed and dried on stretchers in the yard for they were too fragile to iron. We had a large garden that provided us with food, some of which we canned for our winter supply. The garden had to be hoed and weeded. Many a day I spent on the rows of spinach, Swiss chard, and carrots for five cents an hour, money to be hoarded to buy penny candies at the corner store in winter. In September we dug up the potatoes and sent them in barrels to our winter home in Boston.

Father was a busy Boston lawyer, involved in many civic projects. Every weekday during the summer he took a trolley ride from the corner to the station, where he boarded the train for Boston. Sometimes at night we would drive the horse and buggy to meet him on his return. We were always thrilled to see the steam engine come down the tracks. The shrill of the whistle and smoke pouring from the smokestack were exciting events.

In summer my older brother became a "lobsterman," setting his traps out at dawn. I often met him on his return as he rode the waves. I would grab the rope he threw and then help to put the "rollers" underneath in rotation, as we pushed and shoved to roll the boat up above high tide. He had a half-sunken craft in the bay where he stored most of the lobsters. He sold his catch at great profit over the Labor Day weekend, putting a sign on the wall behind the fish houses. Only once did he take me out with him, near Godfrey's Ledge, where the seas were rough. I never asked to go again.

Our young lives were so different from those of the youth of today. We had no radio or television, no automobiles or movies. With little outside diversion, we were free to make our own amusements with whatever we had at hand. In summer our barn was the gathering place for neighborhood friends. We had a large building, with hay in the loft and pigs in the basement. In between were horse stalls, rooms for the "hack," and a wing for the coachmen.

When my older brother and I were very young, we played and fed the horses from the grain bin. We jumped in the hay, played hide-and-seek or cops and robbers, and climbed the "secret" shaft up from the pigpen into the loft. Our friends never found us. Occasionally we played house in a large storage room in the basement of the barn. At this earliest stage I was the only girl and thus the mother. We liked to fill a clothes-basket with hay for a baby but found ourselves in a dilemma about how to produce one. We would find one, somehow. And if we didn't like it, we would throw it down the toilet at home or dispose of it in the outhouse behind the barn. When our friend Willie, the son of the eminent brain surgeon, Dr. Harvey Cushing, came back from inquiring of his father how to obtain a child, the method reported was so repulsive that I refused to go along. This part of our housekeeping ended.

As we grew older, the boys and girls seemed to separate. Instead of playing with dolls, we girls attired ourselves as adults. Our friend Willie and his three sisters lived close to the beach and shoreline road. Mary, the oldest, became my friend. With two other girls from the hotel, we dressed in clothes from the Cushing family's closets and mimicked strolling lovers. Mary and I were the "boys" and the other two our "girlfriends." Parading up and down the boardwalk, we drew many a smile from passing motorists as the girls wobbled along on their high heels. This game did not go on for long; Mary's mother had other ideas.

Years later, when I was busy pursuing my studies and a career, Mrs. Cushing launched her daughters into society. A formidable, domi-

neering woman, she was successful in marrying the three to promi-
nent and wealthy New Yorkers: Mary first to Vincent Astor, then to
James Fosburgh, the painter; Betsey, the middle girl, married James
Roosevelt, and later, Jock Whitney; Babe, the youngest, wed Stanley
Mortimer and then William Paley of CBS fame. My early playmate,
Willie, their older brother, met an untimely end. While a student at
Yale University, he was killed in an automobile accident.

In 1933, when I was a visiting scientist at a geology meeting in
Washington, our group was invited to a reception at the White
House. "Madame" Roosevelt, the President's mother, and Betsey
were our hostesses. President and Mrs. Roosevelt had other, more
urgent duties. When I reached Betsey in the long receiving line and
reminded her of the beach days at Little Boar's Head, she grasped
my hand. As others pressed behind us, she confessed that I was the
only person she had met in the string of guests to whom she could
say anything but "How do you do!"

⟨

If the weather was fair we spent our mornings at the beach, where
we made sand castles and learned to swim in the cold water.
Afternoons were at Rocky Beach, where we explored the tide pools
and hunted for crabs, "Chinamen's caps," and anemones. We
enjoyed running across the slippery rocks and climbing the large
boulders. On the one known as Sugar Loaf we waited until the tide
came in and "timed" the waves to make it to shore without getting
wet. The various outcrops of rocks intrigued me. Father tried to
explain the black dikes and white streaks, which I later learned were
intrusives.

We children became expert on our feet, developing a balance
that stood me well over the years. None of us had bad falls. It was
Mother who slipped one day and sprained her ankle. The gardener
of a woman who lived in a large house overlooking Rocky Beach
drove her home in his wagon, managing to get his horse and buggy
down the steep, rough access used by the farmers to cart seaweed for
fertilizer for their gardens. Mother's ankle was so painful that she
couldn't bear weight on it, but the doctor said it was only a sprain; all
she needed was exercise and massage. A Swedish woman came from
Boston to do the manipulation. It was two months of excruciating
pain before she could walk. Years later, when she was having X rays
for some foot trouble, the doctor looked at the images and asked
when she had broken her ankle.

Mornings, Mother could usually be found busy in the kitchen. As the vegetables ripened, she supervised the elaborate canning operation. Lightning jars had to be sterilized, beans and peas blanched. The stove was kept stocked with coal. Jelly was made from the Concord grapes we gathered along the roadside. The dark-blue grapes smelled delicious as they stewed. We made juice by straining the pots of cooked grapes over buckets covered with linen sieves held aloft by precariously balanced strips of wood.

Even eggs were preserved in "waterglass" for the winter. Because she was so busy with household chores, Mother didn't have much time left to spend with us children. She was exhausted by nightfall. It was Father who told me bedtime stories. I liked to hear most about two gray squirrels named Jack and Billy, and their marvelous adventures all over the world.

One summer at the beach two women swam out too far and were prevented from returning to shore by the undertow. Father went out and held them afloat until a rowboat was obtained from the fish houses near by. Two strong men lifted the women aboard and rowed them to the shore, where they were resuscitated and taken to the hotel by carriage. A couple of weeks later when they came to call, they gave Father a gold fountain-pen in gratitude.

The most cherished memories of my early days were visits to my grandparents' house in North Andover, Massachusetts. To all the children my grandfather was "Grampa," my grandmother "Gramma." The sight of the tall elms of the driveway shading the big, yellow house always gave me a thrill. I remember climbing the steps and entering, first passing through the little room where people left their rubbers and umbrellas. I would then be greeted by the smell of apples stored in barrels in the cellar, suffusing the air in the wide carpeted hall. I liked to rush to see the two huge floor-to-ceiling mirrors, which the kids used for preening and dancing and mimicking each other.

On the left were three living rooms. The first was very fancy, with gilded furniture and cabinets full of china and knickknacks. This room was for special guests only. The second or middle room was for common use. It had a large fireplace and a huge window with a view of the gray branches of an ancient beech tree. The third, with a roaring fire in the fireplace, was exclusively for Grampa. Here, he could smoke his cigar and lounge in his black, upholstered easy chair. This room was off limits for children.

Mother, aunts, and uncle at Gramma's house, North Andover, ca. 1895

In the dining room on the right, there was a large mahogany table, which could seat a dozen. My mother told us how as a girl she had seen a magician at a children's party place a white cloth on a table on which he piled some heavy objects. When he pulled, out came the cloth, with everything else intact. One day Mother persuaded her middle sister to perform this feat of magic for their younger brother. A white damask cloth had been left on the dining-room table after lunch. The girls helped their brother climb up on top and yanked, with dire results: an injured child lay on the floor. I never knew what punishment was meted out.

At the end of the hall was the stairway banister, its gleaming mahogany rail curving upward to the height of the second floor. When no adult was around, our secret delight was a quick slide from the curving top to the bump at the bottom.

In the earliest years, when Gramma and Grampa stayed in North Andover until Christmas, all the family came for the holidays. Seventeen of us were stashed away in double beds and cots in drafty rooms that seemed to stretch on forever. Since the two bathrooms were inadequate, we children were allowed to go down a long corridor to the maids' quarters. Here, we delighted in taking a bath in a battered tin tub.

My grandparents' kitchen was huge, its burning stove always covered with steaming iron pots. Beyond the kitchen a cold hallway led directly to the sheds, a great convenience in winter. A door on the left opened to a "five-holer," with openings graduated in size. The largest was for Grampa, the next one for Gramma, and so on, down to the smallest hole for the baby. I always wondered if they really ever used them all at the same time.

I can recall the endless meal at Christmas, tables overflowing with delicious foods. Afterward, Gramma would line up all fifteen of her children and grandchildren according to age, with the baby of the family at the tail. As we filed past, she handed each one of us a twenty-dollar gold piece. Ours were immediately taken away by my father to add to our bank accounts. Then we were off to the living rooms. The doors between the three had been opened wide to provide space for everyone. As soon as the Christmas tree candles were lighted, we opened our presents. A large bucket of water and a dry mop always stood nearby to douse any flame set by the candles. When things quieted down and the elders sipped their coffee, we youngsters had the run of the house. We played hide-and-seek, crawling under the large beds and squeezing into the closets filled with all kinds of mysterious garb. Later, the kerosene lamps would be illuminated and off to bed we went, our mothers leading the way with candles that made ghost-like shadows on the walls.

The high point of my trips to Gramma's in the fall was a visit to the nearby farm where my cousins lived. It was a long, dusty walk, with ragweed dotting the road. The farmhouse was old, built by my ancestors in the 1700s, with sheds and barns stretching out beyond the low kitchen wing. I would listen for the shrill cry of the peacock telling me that I was almost there. The peacock was a constant presence. He would preen his feathers as he strutted around on the mill wheel, a granite stone that graced the front yard under a huge elm tree. Some of the cousins would join me to see the animals — horses, bull, chickens, and ducks. In the afternoon, when the cows came in from the fields and drank at the trough, I would watch the farmhands milking. Sometimes I was allowed to milk a docile one. The cats stood around waiting for their bowls. One clever feline would sit alert, eager for a stream of milk to be shot into his mouth by one of the milkers.

Best of all the animals was Muggles, the gentle brown pony. He was our plaything and it was on his back that I learned to ride. We washed and curried him, fed him cloverleaf, and rode. He would become ornery as we put on his bridle. Then we mounted, bareback of course. With a few blows from a willow switch he would be persuaded to take his rider out on the road. Muggles was stubborn.

Many a time when I turned him back toward home, he would take the bit in his mouth, give a slight buck, and tear back to the barn, leaving me to walk back in disgrace. I always tried again.

The older boys would take off at a run to get chestnuts in a faraway field. We younger ones tagged along and helped in knocking down the prickly nuts, throwing sticks and rocks to dislodge them. Then we gathered them up in baskets to crack open later on the millstone at the house. But first, we had to swing from the birches. We would shimmy up a likely tree and jump out, holding on to the top tightly with our hands, hoping that it would bend and swing us to the ground.

At the end of one such day I plodded back up the hill, tired and sneezing. I awoke that night with a bad case of asthma. In those days they knew nothing about allergies and hay fever: I was declared sick with bronchitis and the doctor was called. Since I was running a slight fever, he prescribed mustard plasters, great sheets of which were placed on my chest and back. I was then moved to the large double bed in the room that had once been my mother's. While I convalesced, Aunt Harriet, my mother's sister, taught me to sew. I made a sampler, employing all the stitches she knew. Out came some of the stitches if, woe to me, they were not even. I recovered my health fairly quickly, however, being away from the ragweed, cats, and horses.

Toward evening I would often sit on a straw mat that covered the floor of Gramma's small upstairs sitting room and build castles with the large ancestral blocks kept for the grandchildren. Gramma would sew by the fire and ask me to thread her needle. As darkness approached, I would snuggle beside her, and say, "It is growing dark, Gramma." Then she would get up, put down her sewing, light the kerosene lamp, and return to tell me stories of her childhood.

Gramma was a tiny, energetic woman, five feet tall and ninety pounds. She braided her hair, coiling it around her head in a circle. It was grayish white with a touch of red. When she let it down at night, it was long enough to sit on. Her secret was cutting off an inch each month when the moon was full.

Grampa, in contrast, was six feet tall, an imposing, stern-looking figure when he set off for the office wearing his black homburg. His word was law. No one was allowed to criticize his eating habits. We watched in awe as he would consume a large stack of pancakes at breakfast. I would stare as he "slurped" his coffee from a saucer specially designed with extended sides to keep his whiskers dry.

In the fall I would help pick the apples. Many an hour I spent filling the barrels to be stored in the cellar. And, of course, I would climb the trees. Tiring of this, I would go down to the "joggling" board at the edge of the flower garden. Made of fourteen feet of sturdy oak, the board was supported at both ends by a kind of sawhorse, with two sets of steps so the board could be raised or lowered. If cousins appeared, it would be used as a seesaw. But best of all, I spent hours joggling alone, jumping up and down to what seemed great heights.

But soon my fun would end; school was to start. I would spend my last night at Gramma's counting the hours, as the church bell struck the hour and half hour. As dawn approached, I would hear the roosters announcing the new day with their shrill "cock-a-doodle-doo." They called good morning to each other across the fields and crowed good-bye as I prepared for my return to Boston.

Kay dressed for a stroll down Commonwealth Avenue, Boston, 1905

Quarantined in the Attic

F OR THE FIRST six years of my life, we spent winters in Boston in a five-story brick house on Newbury Street. Auntie lived with us in a room on the third floor. Auntie had been with my father since their parents' death, even accompanying Father and Mother on their honeymoon. She herself had never married.

The house included a small downstairs living room, where guests were entertained at tea, and a large dining room beyond, with a dumbwaiter or "lift" to the large kitchen in the basement. The kitchen backed on a small enclosure paved with brick. Since this part of Boston was built on filled land, the cellar was above ground. In those days of famine in Ireland, we were able to employ a cook and an "upstairs" or "parlor" maid to clean and wait on table. We had two sisters who thought themselves lucky to be fed and have a roof over their heads.

At Newbury Street the second floor had a large living room at the front, with Father's and Mother's rooms at the back. My room was in the attic along with the maids' quarters. Father would always read to me at night. One evening he bundled me in blankets and led me out on the small balcony by the bay window. Here, I watched the clouds of smoke from the Chelsea Fire. The whole town went up in flames. I was too sleepy to be frightened, but the picture remains clear in my memory. This was 1908, the last year we lived downtown.

Although he was a busy lawyer, Father was also a very charitable man. As Boston's Overseer of the Poor for twenty-eight years, he refused to be paid, turning his salary back to the city. He also founded a shelter for the homeless. His philosophy was simple: no one should accept charity without contributing something in return. The men could chop wood; the women could perform housework in payment for a night's lodging. He disapproved of "free" turkey dinners, maintaining that many of the men spent their week's allowance on drink. It was Father's belief that some came for a free meal, while their families went without.

Father was very strict and the family disciplinarian. "Spare the rod and spoil the child" was his motto. One particular incident still stands out in my mind. I must have been four and unable to make the bathroom in time. Trying to conceal the evidence, I slid down the two flights of red carpeted stairs on my bottom, thinking I could dry out. Instead, I was crimson in back. For this crime I received a sound spanking and was sent to bed in my attic room, with only crackers and milk for supper. As we got older, we began to resent this treatment. I still get angry when I recall my punishment. At some point my older brother told me he took Father's yardstick, broke it in pieces, and scattered it along the streets of Roxbury as he bicycled to school.

Mother was always busy running the household and caring for the children. My earliest recollection of her at Newbury Street was pushing the baby carriage with my younger brother down Commonwealth Avenue, with me on roller skates clinging to the side. The skates were a gift from Auntie who, against my mother's wishes, had taken me downtown by trolley to the Jordan Marsh department store. Mother felt I was much too young and feared I might fall and get hurt. I first learned how to skate in Auntie's carpeted room.

I had insisted on going with Mother that day to show off my skills. Having had only a week's practice, I was exhausted by the time we reached my favorite statue of a hunting dog, which guarded the front door of one of the Commonwealth Avenue "mansions." After hugging my stone friend, I started back, dragging myself along. Mother objected to my holding onto the carriage. We were both tired out from our excursion.

On reaching home, I was flushed and tired and refused my lunch. Alarmed, Mother took my temperature. Scarlet fever was the doctor's verdict and thus began my banishment to the attic for six long weeks. Before people entered my sick bay they had to go through an anteroom, where they shed their outer clothes, donned white robes, covered their heads with a cloth, and disinfected their hands. This precaution was to prevent my two brothers from catching my disease. I was finally allowed to return to the family when the skin had been completely shed from my body. But none of my prized possessions could be saved. The room had to be fumigated. All my paper dolls were sent to the Children's Hospital contagion ward. It took me days to organize. I put the dolls in separate envelopes and with much difficulty printed the name of each one on the outside. (Father had just taught me to write the letters of the alphabet.) Even my toy teddy bear had to be taken away; fumigation and boiling were not sufficient to save him. I was brokenhearted. The only things I rescued were my goldfish, which were dumped into a tub full of water and deemed "pure."

Auntie was blamed for my condition. According to my mother, I must have caught scarlet fever on the skate-buying excursion. I think this was the turning point in their relationship. Mother wanted a home of her own and demanded that we go further out, to the Fenway, away from Auntie's bad influence. The next fall we moved. Auntie remained in the house on Newbury Street. She must have missed Father terribly. Rather than living alone, Auntie opened her home to needy children from the country, inviting them to live with her during the winter while they attended school in Boston. Since she had no children of her own, in this way she "adopted" at least four.

I missed Auntie. The stories about her are legion. She had built a "bungalow" a half mile from our summer house at Little Boar's Head and would often arrive while we were eating breakfast to see Father before he went to Boston for the day. She would read him a few letters or a poem that had caught her fancy. Then she would take out a bran muffin from her basket. She never ate at our table. Her basket also contained some flowers that she had clipped from neighbors' hedges along the way to our house. On occasion she gave a few to Mother before she left. Sometimes she stopped on her return trip to give a bunch to the neighbors from whom they had been taken. Despite our move to the Fenway, Auntie remained a strong influence in my life. She used to tell me tales of her travels to Egypt and other exotic places. She was even thrown from a donkey in Palestine. I think I owe part of my wanderlust to Auntie's influence.

Grade One, Longwood School, Brookline, 1908. Kay is third child in third row from left. Two girls in row ahead of her are twins with whom she would later climb the Eiger in the Swiss Alps

To the Fenway

A S PART OF his many responsibilities, Father was a trustee for the Sears estate. Mr. Sears had left the city of Boston a small block of brick buildings in the Fenway. Father knew they were for rent. After leaving Newbury Street we moved to the southerly one of the four ivy-covered structures, Number One Plymouth Street. It was much like a town house of today. Mr. Sears had also left a plot of land across the street as a small park for the neighborhood. Unfortunately, he did not know to bequeath it "in perpetuity." Years later, when the city of Boston needed money, the land was sold as a parking lot for Temple Israel, which now also occupies the site of the home where we lived for fourteen years. Today, the little park we so loved is an enormous office complex.

After we moved, I spent many hours watching the construction of the red-brick building of the Winsor School across the street from our new home. A great eight-foot-high brick wall was built around the playground in front of our house. In 1910, when I was eight years old, the school was completed. I looked forward to the day when I would be old enough to attend.

The Plymouth Street house had four stories, basement to attic. In our new home we employed three sisters who had just fled the Irish famine. The eldest was the cook, the middle one the upstairs maid, and the youngest our nurse. Mademoiselle, our governess and French teacher, had departed that fall. The sisters and I were assigned to the attic rooms; Mother, Father, and the boys to the second floor. The living room and dining room were on the first floor, and the kitchen and furnace were in the basement. There was no cellar, as the house was in the fens or marshy area and there would be water problems. Many an hour I spent in the kitchen, enthralled by the cook's stories of their farm in Ireland, their animals, and the failure of the potato crop.

As in the Newbury Street house, there was a dumbwaiter to send food from the kitchen to the pantry. The upstairs maid, who was also the waitress, could serve our meals hot with no stairs to climb. One Christmas, when we were entertaining our relatives for dinner, the children took off for their usual hide-and-seek game while the elders sat around drinking their coffee and gossiping. I had the brilliant idea of hiding my six-year-old cousin Everett in the dumbwaiter. I pushed him in and pulled it half way up. In time the rest of us tired of the game and forgot all about Everett. When it was time to go home, he was nowhere to be found. Finally, we heard his screams. We got the scolding of our lives.

Mother was a sun lover and for the sake of our health she decided that glassed-in porches should be added on the south side of the house. The lower porch led off the dining room but could only be used in spring and fall since it was not heated. The middle one was the sleeping area for the boys. On the top was a small porch with a fence and a glassed-in cage with a glass roof for me. Many a night I dashed from my warm bedroom to sleep out there in the cold. I would crawl under the covers, shivering, and finally fall sleep. I certainly didn't get much fresh air: my head was buried under all the layers of blankets I persuaded Mother to provide. One night in 1910, when I was eight years old, I was awakened by my father, wrapped in a blanket, and taken from my glass cage to the west window inside. From there Father pointed out Halley's Comet, explaining this miracle of the skies and musing that I would probably not live to see its next passing. Little did he know the thrill I would have to catch a glimpse seventy-six years later in 1986, when I was eighty-four years old. But at eight, I was not impressed by the star with a tail. I was much too sleepy.

In the mornings I would rush into my warm room and find a large enamel mug of hot water at my door. I would drink and then brave the cold tub that awaited. A quick dip. I never cheated, but I knew the boys did. Then I was ready for a breakfast of steaming oatmeal and off to school.

On Plymouth Street my brothers and I would often sit in a window and watch the world below. We would see the lamplighter come by with his long pole to light the gas streetlights. Sometimes it was an old man pushing a cart and calling, "Rags and bottles. Rags and bottles." Or the one shouting, "Scissors to grind!" On spring days it would be the fishmonger bellowing, "Mackerel! Fresh mackerel! Two for a quarter!"

Each spring brought the "hurdy-gurdy" man. Strident chords from his hand organ heralded his approach. As he came into sight, we would spy a troupe of youngsters following behind. Excited, we would rush outside. He would stop and doff his cap, revealing his dark, curly hair. Then he would lift the hand organ from his shoulder, set it on a stake in front of him, and crank up the music. Perched on top was an appealing little monkey in a dark-blue felt coat with tarnished braid and a cute little red cap on his head. When the music stopped, the monkey would jump down, remove his hat, and hold it out for our pennies. He would even shake hands with us, his cold, skinny paws clutching ours. If Mother had a banana, we would watch as he hurriedly peeled the skin and bit into it. "Gracias," his master would say, as he doffed his hat again, shouldered his organ, and disappeared.

Every morning I walked to the public elementary school in Brookline, across the Muddy River and through the Fenway, accompanied by Father and Rollo, our coal-black cocker spaniel. Then Father would leave me and board the trolley on Beacon Street for his office downtown. Rollo would stand on the sidewalk watching him depart, and then tiring, trot home alone. One day Rollo did not return: I was sure he had been run over or stolen. Father said to be patient and refused to offer a reward in the papers. Three days later a penciled note on a penny postcard arrived with the whereabouts of our missing pet. Father declined to became a partner to this ruse. He wrote back, telling the finders to open their front door; Rollo would come home. Sure enough, the next night Rollo leaped through an open window, dashing down into our basement kitchen, as glad to be back as we were to see him. Rollo got his name from the popular Rollo books, which Father read to me at night. My favorite stories were about Rollo's travels.

On my way home from school I was not allowed to walk alone through the Fenway. There were "bad men" there who would molest little girls and kidnap them. I always came home the long way. I never dared to tell about the man who accosted me at the foot of Chapel Hill near the Longwood railroad station. Instinctively I knew that he was "bad." I was terrified and raced home. For weeks I took a longer way around. Mother chided me for being late. I didn't know how to confess the reason for my tardiness.

In winter our favorite forbidden sport was "punging." We would watch for a likely ride. In time the milkman's or the grocery man's sleigh might come along. Clinging to the back, we would stand on the runners and travel as far from home as we dared or until the driver discovered us and drove us off, flashing his whip in our direction.

Winter was also a time for coasting or skating at a nearby pond. My skates attached to my shoes with screws; some children had leather straps. As we grew older, we had skis, long slats with a strap for our shoes. We loved to slide wildly downhill, always falling in the process. On one occasion I landed on a sharp stump that was not discernible at snow level. I got a nasty hole in my bottom. Mother rushed me on foot to the nearby Children's Hospital on Longwood Avenue. They refused to treat me as I had just turned thirteen and they would not receive patients over twelve. On we walked to the Peter Bent Brigham Hospital, a good half mile away. There, I was laid on a table, where an intern extracted some pieces of dark-blue bloomer from my behind. That was the end of skiing for me. In the late twenties, European skiing was brought to New England by members of the Appalachian Mountain Club who had been to Switzerland or Norway in the winter. New equipment was introduced. I took up the sport again, this time with skis firmly fastened to my boots, and enjoyed the adventure until I was ninety.

Our lives in Boston were a whirl of activity. All year long Father and Mother had many social gatherings. They belonged to a whist club. Sometimes a women's group came to our home in the afternoon. On rare occasions, we would have men and women for an evening card game. Refreshments were served as we children watched from the stairs. In addition to all his other interests, Father was a Shakespeare scholar and president of the Shakespeare Club of Boston, whose members we would entertain at our house.

Every fall and spring a dressmaker came to the house to make clothes for Mother and me. A great unbleached sheet was spread on the floor of the boys' room while the sewing machine was installed by the window. A week of tiresome fittings ensued before the dressmaker departed. Mother completed the elaborate embroidery and finishing touches herself.

When I was a teenager, Mother brought me to the girls' sewing rooms of a trade school for young people in which Father took a civic interest. They made dresses for me, a trying experience. I had to stand for hours. After all, I had to be properly clothed for dancing school. One year I had a lacy "see-through" dress, with different colored slips: one was pink, one blue, and one yellow to wear alternately under the lace. There were wide silk sashes to match and ribbons for my hair. In class, we were lined up in rows, girls on one side, boys on the other. Our teacher, Miss Carrol, stood in the middle, holding up her voluminous skirts as she showed us the steps. Then the boys advanced to the girls and took partners. No wonder I never liked dancing.

Kay with Mother, ca. 1912

Kay with Dandy, Winsor School, 1917

School Days

AT LONG LAST, when I was eleven, I was admitted to the Winsor School. I went to class by walking through a gate in the high brick wall across from our house. Miss Winsor ran the school with an iron hand. She was very deaf and went around with a small box, which she placed in front of us so that we could talk. We had to look neat. In the first four years of the lower school we wore blue pinafores; red stripes showed our class. The uniforms had to be taken home on weekends to be washed and starched. If we arrived Monday morning without a clean pinafore, we were not allowed to go into assembly.

Miss Winsor's custom was to go from room to room carrying a basket with scissors and a ball of string. We wore our hair in pigtails. If she found a girl with loose hair, she took out the string, cut off a section, and tied back the offending locks. Every spring we had "hair day" in retaliation, arriving in class with ringlets and curls and flowing locks. Needless to say, Miss Winsor ignored us.

On April Fool's Day my first year, three of us emptied all the inkwells in our school-room desks and substituted water. Our subsequent punishment involved bringing scrubbing brushes and soap from home. We spent the next three recesses cleaning up the mess we had made in the lavatory. It was lucky we were not expelled.

One year we had sewing. We made enormous white smocks that completely covered our clothes and white caps, which restrained our hair. We wore these outfits the following year when we had cooking. During our lesson on bread making, I forgot to put the yeast in mine. Peggy, our lively classmate, used my dough as a football. What fun we had. Alas, the cooking teacher returned just as Peggy threw the dough to the ceiling, where it stuck. I got "zero" that day.

At Winsor we studied hard and played hard, too. Homework often kept me up until midnight. The curriculum included Latin and two foreign languages as well as two years of science. I liked science best of all. In springtime we walked on stilts on the brick court. When we were older we learned to play hockey and lacrosse. In the winter we swam in a small indoor pool. Outdoors, a wooden chute was built for coasting and the tennis court was flooded for skating.

I distinguished myself at Winsor by going to school for eight years without missing a day. This record was nearly broken in the spring of my senior year when the doctor decided to operate on my nose to cure my hay fever. That Easter vacation I had developed a high temperature and infection. While I lay in Massachusetts General Hospital listening to the noise of the early morning milk trucks as the horses clip-clopped across the cobblestones, my friends visited, alarmed to learn that I would not be well in time to return to school. My perfect record would be broken so near the end. Returning home the night before school started, I was put to bed and told I could not attend the next day. But I was determined. Mother couldn't stop me. The next morning I climbed in the library window at the end of Plymouth Street just in time not to be called "late." I was weak and wobbly. When Miss Winsor heard about my arrival, she ordered me home. I refused. In exasperation, she led me to her room, produced a steamer rug, and put me in a lounge chair on a small porch outside her window. There I had to stay as she watched over me. But I was at school.

Years later, when I gave a talk to the Deaf Guild of Boston about my work in Africa, Miss Winsor came up to me and asked, "Katharine, what did I teach you at my school that made you do the things you have done?" She always felt responsible for the training and future of her students and I had her puzzled. I had no ready explanation, but it was clear that Winsor was an important part of my life.

On Saturdays in the city I went to the Art Museum School, a long walk across the fens. Mother thought I was destined to be an artist. She possessed talent and had painted before her marriage. Or perhaps this was her plan to keep me out of trouble. Each week I spent four hours in my artistic pursuits, the first two in my choice of crafts, jewelry work. I made silver pins and pendants and eventually became so skilled that I was allowed to use gold. The next two hours of the session were in the museum itself where I sat on a stool and drew a charcoal sketch of a sculpture of my choice. My favorite was a horse. I hated those horrid plaster heads of emperors and soldiers. The curious public constantly asked questions about my age or interests. I hated this, too. I was not destined to make art my life's work.

When I was thirteen, I begged my parents to bring my horse Dandy to Boston from our summer home in New Hampshire. He had been a gift from Auntie the year before. She had offered me the choice of a horse or a gold watch for my birthday. Of course, I chose the horse. He was entirely in my charge. I fed, curried, and rode him. In the summer we explored miles of country roads away from the coast and galloped on the beaches at low tide. Because I knew that the horse made me sneeze and wheeze, I was careful to cover my nose with a bandanna in the stable. No one knew about allergies to horses at that time and I was not about to enlighten them. Dandy was broken to carriage as well as to riding. On Sundays in the country we drove the half mile to church. A special wicker protector was placed across the front wheel on the right side of the carriage so Mother would not soil her long skirt when she climbed in. We children crowded in back beside her and Father sat in front to drive.

In Boston I promised to exercise Dandy every day. Father finally relented and drove him down from the beach. Dandy boarded at a stable a mile away from us in nearby Brookline. In June before we all decamped to the seashore, I rode back to the beach with Father in the buggy. We went as far as Ipswich (Massachusetts) the first day and returned home by train. The next day we took the train back to Ipswich and completed the long, dusty ride to the shore, thirty miles in all, along what is now Route One. The drumlins or glacial hills lining the road were steep. I pitied poor Dandy. From time to time I climbed down from the carriage to lighten his load and walked behind in his dust. The road is now tarred and widened, the tops of the hills leveled.

Dandy was stubborn and loved company. If he saw a horse ahead of him, he would dash forward and attach himself to his new friend. His favorite was the one ridden by the mounted policeman. Many an afternoon I rode the rounds with the officer on duty. One day the policeman got a call, delivered by a motorist, to return to an accident in the Fenway. Off he rushed, while I kept Dandy going on ahead until I thought he had forgotten his companion. Not so. As I turned him around, he took the bit in his mouth. I lost control. He raced back across Brookline Avenue to the Village, dodged a street car, and then dashed along the bridle path. He was still galloping as he neared the stable. Running out of control, he turned too soon. When he saw the curbstone, he stopped in his tracks. Off I went. The witnesses who picked me up said I had turned a complete somersault. Dandy went on to the stable, while I walked back in disgrace, bruised, but whole. We never did catch up with the policeman. In the winter months when the bridle path was slippery, Dandy was housed in a riding school with an indoor track to which

I could walk in half an hour. Once in a while if the weather was bad I was given a nickel for carfare. This site is now home to Fenway Park, Boston's beloved baseball stadium. The bridle paths have long vanished.

During World War I there was to be a war bonds parade to stimulate an interest in buying bonds. One of my riding companions asked Father if I might participate. He vowed to watch out for me if I went. Father agreed. The parade was exciting. Dandy behaved himself until we passed the reviewing stand at the state house, where state and municipal dignitaries were presiding. When the band behind us struck up a loud wartime tune, Dandy started to buck and bolt. My protector was able to grab my reins and hold him back. Fortunately, this time I hung on.

During his third year in town, Dandy was showing signs of age and began stumbling. I was thrown into the dirt several times and rescued by concerned motorists. I never told my parents, but the stable man reported Dandy's skinned shins to my Father. This was the end. Dandy was sold.

Riding in the war bonds parade was not my only war-related activity. As a Girl Scout during the years of the First World War, I helped the war effort by folding bandages for the Red Cross — hundreds of them. We also knitted heavy woolen socks for the navy. Because these had no heels, they would fit any of the soldiers.

Father was always very busy with meetings in Boston, even when we moved to the beach in summer. He was chairman of many committees and had been appointed by Mayor Curley to head the Liquor Licensing Commission. In the summer of 1918, before the war ended, Father came home to the beach by train and trolley appearing more tired than usual. The next morning he stayed in bed. Mother was busy canning beans and we children were at the beach. At eleven o'clock Mother went upstairs with some hot chocolate. To her horror, she found Father lying face down on the floor. The shock was great for us all. I had lost my protector, my guide, and my advisor. At first I couldn't accept his death. How could he leave me, I asked. It was Father who had encouraged my studies. If I had a question, it was Father who got me books to find the answers. Auntie tried her hardest to take me into the room where Father was laid out. She said he was beautiful. I refused to look. I mourned quietly, with a lump in my stomach, but no tears.

Many dignitaries attended the funeral in Boston. The casket was covered with flowers. I sat in the front pew, still unable to believe he was gone. But when the casket was opened and people passed by to pay their respects, I saw the tip of my father's nose. I was overcome with grief and at last the unshed tears poured out. My older brother, who was sitting beside me, admonished me to be quiet. It was then that I knew Father was gone.

In 1920, two years after Father's death, I began to prepare for college. I chose Bryn Mawr, the most select of women's colleges in those days. To qualify I had to take special exams. Three of my classmates from Winsor who also hoped to go to Bryn Mawr went along with me. The tests were difficult and were given in various subjects over three years. They were always held over Memorial Day at the old Massachusetts Institute of Technology (MIT) building on Boylston Street, and there was always a parade going by on one of the days. Despite the distraction, I passed. In fact, I won the New England Competitive Scholarship. In the fall of 1921 I was headed for college at Bryn Mawr, having graduated from Winsor with eight years of perfect attendance.

Aerial view of the Eiger route from an old postcard, Switzerland

Summer Climbs

ACH AUGUST from the age of seven to my college days, I was sent to the White Mountains of New Hampshire to improve my health. I will always look back to these summer months with fond memories. My mountain sojourns were often preceded by weeks of sniffling at the seashore: "Katharine's rose cold" it was called, and I sat in misery on the sand, bundled in sweaters beside my mother and her friends while the other children enjoyed the sea and waves. No one knew that Katharine's cold was hay fever. Again in the fall I would sneeze and wheeze until finally the doctor decided that mountain air might cure this sickly child.

So every year, from mid-August until mid-September, a motherly middle-aged widow who spent her vacation in Randolph, New Hampshire, took me in. Here, I was away from ragweed and our animals, which, we did not realize at the time, were the root of all my troubles.

I loved the mountain climbs and walks in the woods. Since I was not allowed to ascend the higher peaks until I was older, I spent my early years following the brooks and lower trails. On my trips I became curious about why the mountains were there, what formed the rocks that were so different from the coastal terrain. I vowed that someday I would study geology and answer these questions. What a great training ground these explorations would prove to be for the years of fieldwork that lay ahead.

I enjoyed staying with my guardian, who was very kind to me. When her new house was being constructed, I was allowed to help the carpenter shingle the roof. When her son and family built their home down the road, I was permitted to shingle again. On a visit years later, they pointed to a brick in the large chimney in the living room. It was askew. "We call this Katharine's brick," they joked. In my youthful zeal I had climbed up the side of the chimney to get to the roof. The cement was not dry and the brick had tilted.

My days in Randolph were also spent bicycling for the mail and reading. I consumed many volumes of Walter Scott and Dickens, which my guardian had in her library, as well as the required books on my school's summer booklist. Each week when I was quite young I walked three miles up the dusty road, carrying my bag of dolls, to play with my nearest friend. In later years a family with daughters about my age came to live in the "Ravine House." Miggy was the one who loved to explore with me. We "stone-hopped" the rocky brook and built huts out of fallen wood.

When I was in my teens and finally allowed to climb mountains, it was Miggy's oldest sister, Isabel, who became my hiking companion. She was my idol. On one expedition we climbed Mount Adams with two older men, who were acquaintances of her family. On our trek we met some friends who owned a hut called Grey Knob, high in the mountains. They invited us to spend the night. Isabel wanted to continue the following day to the top of Mount Washington to meet some of her Bryn Mawr classmates. We borrowed money from our two companions so that we could walk the trail to the railroad with her friends and then return by train. At Grey Knob that night we took our blankets to a rocky perch above the hut and witnessed the most brilliant display of northern lights I have ever seen. In the morning our friends gave us some chocolate bars and raisins for our climb. It was all they could spare.

Off we went to Mount Jefferson, north of Mount Washington. The day was perfect, the view glorious. We decided to drop down into the Great Gulf, then climb up the headwall to the top of Mount Washington, 6,288 feet. By the time we reached a small, frigid lake at the head of the gulf, we were hot and tired. We shed our clothes and went for a quick dip. While ascending the head of the ravine, we both fell ill from all the chocolate and raisins. This slowed us down. At supper in the "Tip-Top" house, where we spent the night, two young men from Yale joined our group. Looking around, they asked if anyone had seen two mermaids swimming in Spaulding Lake in the bottom of Great Gulf. Apparently we had been observed.

On returning to Randolph that night, we were greeted by Isabel's parents, who were much put out by this escapade. My guardian had been frantic. Little did I guess that years later I would return to these same trails and ridges as a partner in mapping the White Mountains.

After graduation from the Winsor School, gone were my carefree summers at the shore and in the mountains. Growing up I had always wanted to go to camp. Here I was at last at Lake Fairlee, Vermont, not as a camper but as an assistant counselor. Since I had learned jewelry work at the museum, I was assigned to help with crafts. So instead of having fun outdoors with the campers, I spent most of the time helping the girls finish their pins and rings for display on Parents' Day. I did, however, have time to swim, passing all the tests to qualify as an instructor. Since I was able to stay up on the aquaplane, in reality a board tied behind a motorboat, I was assigned to the rear position. From here I could instruct the beginners and rescue them if it became necessary.

I was sad, however, that there was to be no horseback riding or mountain climbing for me. But near the end of camp I was allowed to go on an overnight canoe trip on the Connecticut River, where we camped on a floodplain and cooked our meals over an open fire. When evening came, the other female counselors took off for the village with their attractive male counterpart, leaving me in charge of the fifteen girls. Rumor had it that the campers were scheming to "skinny-dip" as soon as I was asleep. I insisted that we go knee-deep only and hold hands. We all had fun and I felt justified in my actions, having kept the girls out of danger. When the head of camp heard about this, I was soundly berated. I was not invited back to camp the next year.

Although I was disappointed that I couldn't return to camp the following summer, fate was on my side. After my freshman year of college Auntie decided I should join her on a "grand tour" of Europe. We traveled with a small group of eight, shepherded by a knowledgeable woman as guide. First we were to take in the museums and castles of England, then on to Paris. On our departure Mother gave me twenty-five dollars for gifts and souvenirs. I expressed a desire to fly the English Channel. Mother put her foot down. It was dangerous, she said.

In Paris I saw an ad for sightseeing from a plane. Here was my chance. I had not promised that I wouldn't take a ride if the opportunity arose. The temptation was too great. I didn't tell Auntie and swore the younger members of our party to secrecy. They promised to cover for me in case I didn't get back in time.

Early the next morning I boarded the bus for Le Bourget Airport. I was told that the plane was a small, open, two-seater, a Handley Page. They would go up if there were two passengers; I was the only one who showed up. Since twenty-five dollars would cover both tickets, I decided to give up buying trinkets. This would be a real souvenir. I handed over all the money I had. In return, I was given a leather jacket, helmet, and goggles. They strapped me in and with a roar the plane took off.

The flight was even more wonderful than I had imagined. I leaned out over the side to gaze into space and at the sights below. We flew low over Notre Dame, the Louvre, and Versailles. Of course, I was late returning for the afternoon excursion. Auntie and the group leader were worried. My co-conspirators could no longer keep my secret. I was severely scolded. But what did I care? I had been on top of the world.

After Paris we went on to Oberammergau in Bavaria to see the Passion Play, which was performed every fourth year. Here we were honored to stay in the home of the "Christus." After, when we reached Mürren in Switzerland, I rebelled. I had had enough with conventional sightseeing. The Alps beckoned. Since Auntie was exhausted, she agreed to stay with me in Mürren for ten days while the others returned to Paris to visit the chateau country.

For my first ascent I chose the Jungfrau. Having found a guide, I set out by train to spend the night at the Jungfraujoch. A young Englishwoman and I were assigned to a bunk near the outhouse facilities. I couldn't sleep. She was in trouble: how could she get out of her corset without standing up? She fidgeted and rolled. I took pity and helped her roll over to unloosen the stays. In the hours before daylight I laced her up again. She would not stir in public without that corset. No respectable woman would. Needless to say, she and her uncle climbed only half way up the mountain.

Early the next morning my guide and I set out by lantern to get ahead of the melting snow. Two Princeton boys and their guides preceded us, the only other climbers that day. My guide saw that they were in trouble at the "Bergschrund," the large crevasse below the summit at the head of the long Aletsch Glacier. We took an alternate route. To their embarrassment, I was sitting on the summit when they arrived.

Back in Mürren I ran into two girlfriends from home, twins from Brookline, who were planning to climb the Eiger, a difficult ascent. Auntie agreed to let me go with them. If Auntie had been younger, she would have climbed, too. The twins had a younger guide, while I had the same steady, older one I had been entrusted to on the Jungfrau. We spent the night in the Eigergletscher hut. At dawn we set out by lantern light with my guide in the lead, followed by the twins next, then their guide. I drew up the rear. Roped together, we were well equipped with ice axes and hobnailed boots. On reaching a chimney as the sun rose in the east, we found it coated with ice. There was no way to proceed. We had to circle by a much longer route on a glacier. It was late when we reached the cone of the moun-

Kay (second from left) with English tourists about to set out on Grindelwald Glacier, Switzerland, Summer 1922

tain. The route was steep and icy and the snow was melting. Steps had to be cut. It was almost one o'clock in the morning by the time we reached the summit. The guides gave us a sip of brandied tea, a piece of cheese, and dry bread. We all huddled together with our axes embedded in the snow. It had been exhilarating but frightening, with several thousand feet of drop on both sides of the cone's narrow ridge of ice. When we rose to go, I pulled out my ice axe; there was light below. I had been sitting on a cornice of overhanging ice, with the Aletsch Glacier far below.

I couldn't wait to get started again. The going was dangerous. Our steps had melted. This time I was fastened in front; the twins' guide came next to cut out new steps, followed by the twins attached close together and my guide as the anchor at the end of the rope. I hoped he could hold us. Slipping and sliding, I was held back by the guide as he cut footholds for the others. With the cone safely maneuvered, we reached the glacier. The snow had melted in the hot sun. I floundered and sank, picking the way. The others bypassed the places where I sank deepest. But still I had to go first. It was getting late as we neared the Eigergletscher hut. A group of guides had come up to meet us bringing lanterns, which they lighted the last half hour as we crossed a rocky scree. Exhausted, we spent the night. There was no telephone to announce our safe arrival.

When we changed trains for Mürren at the Grindelwald Junction, there was a large sign beside a telescope at the station that read, "Sights to be seen today. Three American women and two guides on the Eiger." Our progress had been followed. We were greeted with relief by Auntie and the twins' parents, who had watched through the telescope all day from Mürren. As it turned out, our descent had caused alarm. They had counted only four persons in the group: the twins were roped so close together that they looked like one. The others had kept this news from Auntie, whose eyesight was bad. She never knew that they feared one of us had been lost.

Time was running out on my grand tour; we had to return to Paris. Before we left I was allowed one more mountain; I chose the Breithorn. My trusty guide and I had to walk a long distance. We followed a glacier up to a small hut in a col, where we camped out. Next day I had my first experience rock-climbing on a cliff. I slipped and hung like a spider until my guide hauled me up. The rest of the climb was safe and exciting. From the top I could look down at the world; my infatuation with the Alps had begun.

The summer of my sophomore year of college was quite a different experience. I was hired to be the "athletic chaperone" to three young sisters who had been at camp together, where they had run off to go birding and exploring. The camp could not tolerate this behavior so their mother had rented a cottage in Bristol, Maine, where they were to spend the summer. There they would be allowed to wander at will if accompanied by a suitable companion, one who could cope with their questions. And they wanted answers to everything. Since I had studied biology, geology, and chemistry, and because I loved to explore, I was chosen. I met my charges at Portland, boarding the train in which they had spent the night traveling from Philadelphia. I was immediately put to the test, called on to identify all the flowers we saw from the train window. Since I had made a small herbarium one summer at the Winsor School and had collected more than a hundred varieties of flowers at the beach and in the mountains, I was well prepared.

My charges and I had a rowboat; every day we departed with a picnic lunch to explore the little islands in the bays. We could even skinny-dip since there were no summer tourists with motorboats in those days. We collected flowers and rocks. On one occasion we observed a pair of ospreys raising their young in the top of a dead pine tree. The girls wanted to climb up. I volunteered but was "bombed" by the birds when I reached the nest. We always rowed back through the gut under the little bridge promptly at six o'clock to avoid causing their mother anxiety. At night we slept in cots on a veranda. I had to tell a story before they fell asleep. The one they remembered best was about muzzling sculpins, fish with enormous mouths. I was reminded of the stories my father used to tell me when I was a child.

Part of my job was to tutor the oldest girl in Latin, in the evening, when she was most resistant to learning. She hated it. One night, when she complained of a headache and refused to do any more work, I got a hot-water bottle, filled it with ice, and placed it on top of her head. She and her sisters were convulsed with laughter. I had won; she grudgingly translated a few sentences. That fall she managed to pass her make-up exam. By summer's end a lifelong friendship was formed.

Bryn Mawr College May Day Programme, 1924
Courtesy, Bryn Mawr College Archives

Bryn Mawr

L EAVING NEW ENGLAND for the first time to go to Bryn Mawr College in Pennsylvania in 1921 was rather overwhelming for a girl brought up in a sheltered, unsophisticated atmosphere in Boston. But I soon adjusted to the college routine. Every freshman was required to have an interview with President Thomas. "PT" as she was known, was an imposing, no-nonsense, rather terrifying woman. She asked what I planned to take as a major. When I answered biology and geology, she commented, "Well, you are the first student to come to me who has already made up her mind." She seemed pleased.

To fulfill all the necessary requirements, I had to take biology and chemistry my first year, then geology the second. This was disappointing since I was anxious to get started on the study of the whole earth process. The head of Bryn Mawr's small geology department was Florence Bascom, known to all as Flossie. She was then the most outstanding woman geologist in the United States and had trained the few women who were entering into a field previously filled by men alone. Since she was taking a sabbatical leave the next year, I had to begin my studies under a delightful man from the West Coast who was retired from the geological survey. Dr. W. S. Tangier Smith turned out to be an inspiration. He was not familiar with the Philadelphia area, so two of us students volunteered to go out with him to scout places for field trips. Our first excursion was to a cemetery down the road from the college. Here, I discovered, a great deal can be learned from tombstones.

Since we had no cars, we walked many miles to find suitable outcrops to study. Dr. Smith was often able to get a bus to take the students to several distant localities. Here again, he helped unravel the stories that the rocks revealed. Some of his ideas differed from those of Flossie. These divergences later generated a lively discussion. She always ended the argument, "The trouble with you is that you started geology the wrong year!"

As a freshman, I was at the beck and call of every sophomore, a kind of hazing designed to put us in our places. We performed errands or other simple tasks and were often called on to "exchange" with one of their friends for lunch or dinner. And they had many friends. I would be sent to some other dormitory to eat, while a friend would come to mine. Many days I was kept on the run, back and forth between buildings. I rarely ate with my own friends.

On Freshman Night in the spring we could retaliate for all the inconveniences we had endured. We were a "red" class and had a tradition to live up to. A previous red class had taken all the sophomores' corsets and tied them high on the maple trees in Senior Row. The Haverford men swarmed to the Bryn Mawr campus that day.

With my close friend Elaine as co-conspirator, I spent hours arranging the tricks we would do to annoy those pestering sophomores. We had three hours to prepare while they were at their annual banquet. First, we made dummies of our enemies and laid them out in a morgue on the first floor. We then composed poems that included anything derogatory we could think of and placed them on the mannequins. The sophomore leader was the class policeman, so from the chandelier in the middle of the hall we hung her effigy toting a policeman's billy, which we had borrowed from a cooperative college guard.

We also hung festoons of the sophomores' silk stockings over the banisters to the different floors. (We had the foresight to put tiny name labels in the toe of each, so they could be returned to the owners later.) We put Epsom salts in the water coolers and Vaseline on the toilet seats. We marked the transoms of the sophomores' rooms with red devil cutouts.

Early that morning I had gathered arms full of skunk cabbage leaves and hid them until the time came for placing them on the floor of each girl's room. In chemistry we had found a certain medicinal powder that was obnoxious, but harmless. We scattered some of this on the skunk cabbage leaves. When the sophomores snatched up the leaves, the powder was spilled. The odor remained in the dormitory for years.

But our most outrageous prank was placing a small, live, greased pig under a bureau drawer in the room of the sophomore who had hounded us the most. We had rented the creature from a nearby farmer, who arrived with it promptly at six in the evening at the front gate of the college. Elaine and I dragged the pig in a crate across the campus and hid it in my bedroom until the appropriate time. When the sophomores were at dinner we carried the swine into the chosen room and greased it with Vaseline. When the pig was discovered, it was chased from floor to floor until a kindhearted junior, who sided

Kay with class ball as captain of the freshman Bryn Mawr water polo team, 1922

with us, caught the animal and put it in its crate on the fire escape outside her window.

Elaine and I were sure we would be in trouble as we were the "plotters"; our classmates merely helped. We knew there would be an enormous uproar and we planned our escape. Without telling a soul, we took blankets and climbed out a small window on the top floor to the roof. There, behind a gable, we spent the night. Needless to say, they knew who the culprits were. But no one could find us. We had not signed out for "overnight" in the required record book. This misdemeanor alone exacted punishment.

When President Thomas heard about our outrageous behavior, she thought it deserved expulsion. To our good fortune, a junior in our dormitory, who was head of Self-Government, argued our case. Technically, we had really been in the dormitory even though it was on the roof. It must have been our youth and pent-up spirits that made us mischievous, she explained. We were given a second chance. We were lucky.

The following year Elaine departed to another hall. Freshman year I had also made friends with Dot from Baltimore. She was petite and dainty, in contrast to me, a strong Yankee. Opposites somehow get on well together. Sophomore year I moved to a tiny room under the eaves on the top floor of the dormitory. Dot and I spent many an hour there fighting the Civil War. The attic had only four bedrooms, the remainder being the trunk room, with a rope elevator outside our doors to bring up the trunks. Nate, a classmate with whom we had become good friends, had a large room across the way. We held parties there whenever she received crates of pretzels and baskets of fruit and cakes from her relatives. We also had tea or "muggle," a thick concoction made up of cocoa and condensed milk added to boiled water.

Since Dot and I were not going home for Thanksgiving, Nate invited us to her home in Wilmington. We were unprepared for the meal, a lavish feast in the large dining room, served by uniformed servants. The family was seated around a huge table, with Nate's father at the head and her stepmother at the foot. Arranged on both sides were their six children. Dot and I were placed opposite each other. The first course was raw oysters on the half shell. Dot and I looked at each other across the table and grimaced. Suddenly, the smallest boy, who was sitting next to his father, pointed to us and said in a loud voice, "But they aren't eating their oysters!" He was promptly countermanded, "Oh! But you must eat yours. They are guests and may do as they please." We turned crimson, each trying to swallow an oyster to no avail. They were slippery and slimy. Repulsive! We managed to get through the rest of the five courses with no untoward incidents.

Dot took charge of my life. She saw that I got to bed at ten when I was in training for one of the athletic teams, which was often. Thanks to my Winsor School training I excelled in sports. I alternated each year as captain of the swimming or water polo team.

Our dormitory, Merion Hall, was a firetrap. Four flights of wooden steps led up to our rooms. The elevator shaft was beside our rooms. We had frequent fire drills. Outside my window was a metal ladder leading down five flights to the basement. It was imperative that we be able to use the ladder in case of fire. Dot maintained that she would never dare. When I became fire captain my junior year, I decided to have an unannounced drill so that everyone on the upper floors would have to go down the fire escapes. I pulled the alarm late one afternoon when the students were in their rooms changing for dinner. Since I knew Dot was in her room, I arranged to be upstairs too. I climbed down the fire escape, with Dot following behind. I felt relieved that she had made the descent; in the event of a real fire, she wouldn't panic. The fire escape on the other side of our building had a platform at the end of the ladder that was supposed to let down with a person's weight. It simply fell off when a girl stepped on it. Fortunately, she had hold of the upper railing and was not injured. All the fire escapes were inspected after this near catastrophe.

Our sophomore year Dot and I were taking physiology. When she was presented with a slimy frog to dissect, she panicked. There was no way she could pith it. I sympathized and performed the procedure for her and for one or two other friends who were struggling with theirs. Although the frog was dead, the heart still beat for several days. We dissected the creature and tied threads to the arteries around the heart, which was then hung in a saline solution with the strings attached to rotating drums covered with carbon paper. This arrangement gave us a continuous record of the heartbeat. We added various drugs to the solution to measure their effect on the heart. Although Dot did not go on to take pre-med as she had planned, I had made a lifelong friend. Whenever she travels and sees a frog, silver or bronze or even a postcard, she sends it to me. I return in kind on all occasions.

Every four years at Bryn Mawr there is a large May Day celebration with a colorful Elizabethan pageant. We spent our entire junior year preparing for this event. Each dormitory was assigned to make a certain number of paper flowers, which then were used to decorate the May queen, the pair of horses that pulled the cart in which she rode, and her entourage of attendants. The allotment for the four of us on the top floor came to a hundred flowers a week. Usually we made daffodils and tulips, spending hours at work in Nate's room. Everyone was involved and the task cemented many a friendship.

May Day itself was a glorious celebration, with visitors coming from far and wide. First came the parade, with two oxen pulling a cart with the largest of several maypoles decorated with gaily colored streamers. The May queen came next in an old cart festooned with garlands of flowers. The dancers followed. Plays were performed at various campus locations. Everyone had a part. I was supposed to be a morris dancer but at the last minute I was assigned the part of Aristotle in a play entitled *Alexander and Campaspe* by John Lyly. I delivered four incomprehensible philosophical phrases, which I can no longer recall.

But of course Bryn Mawr was not all pranks and pageants. We studied hard, late into the night. I especially loved Latin. One day in class we were translating Ovid by sight. No dictionaries were allowed. When the word "gallina" appeared, the professor expressed doubt of anyone knowing the definition. I correctly answered "chicken." She eyed me suspiciously, thinking I had a trot or translation in my lap. "How did you know that?" she asked. I replied that as a child I had two cherished stuffed animals, one a pachyderm quadruped, the other a gallinaceous biped. I got an A in the course. Perhaps my father's early teaching was paying off.

Travel back and forth to Bryn Mawr between Philadelphia and Boston was by night sleeper. At Christmas vacation one year, on our way to Boston, our train hit a freight car outside New Haven. My Dedham (Massachusetts) classmate and I were thrown against the headboard of our bunks. We rushed out to find the engine and baggage car overturned, enveloped in steam. The occupants had been killed. Our sleeping car was near the middle; we had been lucky to escape serious injury. We sat in the cold cars from the middle of the night until late afternoon when the blocks of granite scattered about from the freight were removed and the overturned cars righted. Our families were waiting for us at the Boston station, much concerned about our safe return.

At the end of the school year I had wanted to take the Merchants' and Miners' boat from Philadelphia to Boston. Mother thought it dangerous. But after the Christmas locomotive wreck, I considered it was much safer than travel by train. Without telling our families, a friend and I decided to take the boat. We boarded in high spirits. Sometime in the middle of the night we were awakened by a thump and much calling and yelling on deck. We went up, only to find that we had run aground not far from Woods Hole on Cape Cod. At daybreak we were given the choice of going ashore in a tender, traveling by rail to Boston, or waiting for the morning tide to float the ship. We chose to stay.

The whole morning was full of activity. Tugs arrived but they were unable to float the boat. Perhaps at high tide that night the vessel could be freed from the rock that held it. Again, we waited. A motorboat came alongside late that afternoon with a telegram demanding that we return to Boston at once. Our families had read about the accident in the afternoon paper and saw our names listed as passengers. But it was too late. There was no train to Boston at that time; we telegraphed back that we were safe and would continue our journey.

Late that night, they freed the ship. With a hole in the hull it had to be taken to Martha's Vineyard for repairs. The purser told us to return by ferry from Oak Bluffs to Woods Hole the next morning. There, he accompanied us to the train station, paid for our tickets, and went along all the way to Boston. Needless to say, our families were eagerly awaiting our arrival. We were scolded, but we were safe.

Upon entering my junior year of college, I decided to double up on geology courses and take some advanced classes with the graduate students. To do this, I had to get Flossie's approval when I returned in the fall. Before school opened that year, I had been to hockey camp in the Pocono Mountains and slipped on wet grass, catching myself on my right hand and breaking the bones. Arm in sling, I presented myself to Flossie, who gave me one look and said, "Well! You don't expect to become a geologist starting out with your arm in a sling?" I could have dropped through the three floors to the basement of Dalton Hall. She did grant the permission.

Flossie proved to be a stern teacher, discouraging the students from pursuing geology. She had had a very uphill battle pushing her way into a man's field. For her there could be no compromise. With my right hand incapacitated, I asked about putting off the inking of a large circle in my study of a topaz crystal; she refused. The circle was projected on a large sheet of paper from an instrument called the hand circle contact-goniometer. I struggled, unsuccessfully, to ink the design with my left hand. When Flossie left the room, one of the graduate students took pity and finished it for me.

While pursuing the study of geology I was also doubling up my courses in biology, still torn between medicine and rocks. On one occasion I had caught a bat in the chemistry room and was studying its kidney cells from thin sections, which involved placing them on glass plates and setting them in bottles of xylol mixtures. These solutions had to be changed quite often so I lined up the bottles on the window sill in front of my microscope in the geology lab. One day Flossie came in, saw the bottles, and asked what they were. She pronounced that I would never become a geologist if I put up with all these distractions.

Quite discouraged with Flossie's attitude, I decided to apply to Woods Hole for the summer course in invertebrate zoology. There were five of us taking pre-med and we all applied, knowing that only one place would be given to a Bryn Mawr student. I was quite open in my application, clearly stating my conflicting interests. To the dismay of the other applicants, I was accepted. The other four became doctors and never forgave me.

The summer course was very concentrated. We had classes in the morning and field trips in the afternoons. It took me back to summers on Rocky Beach. But now I was finding out about things I never knew existed, things even Father could not have taught me. On Sundays I enjoyed exploring the neighboring islands. Friends and I rented a boat to cross the gut. One day, as we started to row across, a large ferry from New York came down the channel, right in our path. One of my friends from Ohio had never learned to swim and we had no life preservers. For a few dreadful moments I rowed like fury. People on the ship were lined up along the rails to watch us. They knew we wouldn't make it. There was nothing for us to do but drift with the current and hope we wouldn't be hit. Luckily, we slipped along the bow in the wake of the boat and didn't capsize in the rough swells it made. Everyone on board cheered. Years later my daughter took a course in biology at Mount Holyoke College taught by that same Ohio friend. When she learned that Betty was my daughter, she recounted the incident and described how I had saved her life at Woods Hole.

The Woods Hole summer whetted my appetite to explore my surroundings. Fascinated by earth science, I returned with great enthusiasm to Bryn Mawr for my senior year. I vowed not to let on to Flossie that I had chosen a career in geology. I wanted to do this on my own, allowing her to continue to think that biology was my real field. I knew that if I were to become a geologist, I had to find out if I could compete in a man's world. Without consulting Flossie, I applied to the University of Wisconsin for a graduate fellowship. To my delight, I was awarded the geology-geography fellowship for 1925–1926.

My Steps Lead West

THE SUMMER BEFORE graduate school, I made plans to see as much of the West as I could before classes began in the fall. I decided to broaden my perspective of the United States, to expand upon my East Coast studies, which seemed very localized and narrow. The University of Wisconsin offered a three-week summer course in the physiography of the Front Range in Colorado run by Professor Lobeck, who was a genius at interpreting the region through sketches and diagrams drawn on a small blackboard that he carried.

The session began at Rocky Mountain National Park and continued north by train with several stops, one at Yellowstone National Park, finishing at Glacier National Park in Montana. I had also signed up for a field course at the University of Colorado that would not start until August, which gave me time between sessions to make a circle of the California coast. My itinerary included excursions to Mount Rainier and Crater Lake and a visit to the University of California at Berkeley. The train schedules showed that I could even take in Yosemite.

When the Wisconsin field trip broke up at Glacier Park, I headed west by train accompanied by Flo, a student from Rochester, who had decided to climb Mount Rainier with me. A bus took us from Seattle to Paradise Inn high in the national park. We arrived to find snow still lying about in piles. We were outfitted for the climb with paraffin-soaked pants, the waterproofing of the day, and given hobnailed boots, goggles, and an ice axe. Our faces were to be painted with zinc oxide, pink or white, our choice. Joining us on the climb were two barbers from Seattle, a minister from Chicago, and a guide. For the start of the ascent, we were all lined up in front of the inn at three in the afternoon, photographed, and given a lecture by the director. "We pride ourselves on groups reaching the summit," he said. "Remember, the last thousand feet are the hardest." These words stuck in my mind.

Off we went. Three hours of easy climbing would bring us to a small hut, where we would spend the night. A mile from the cabin Flo was hit by altitude sickness and had to be supported the rest of the way. Arriving at our destination, we put her in the long bunk and the guide massaged her feet. She revived but there was no question

Summit of Mount Rainier, Summer 1925. From left, barbers, Kay, minister

of her climbing with us the next day. She could sleep late and await our return.

In the cold, early dawn we departed, single file. As the cone steepened, it became encrusted with snow. The guide hitched us together; he led the way while I brought up the rear. The altitude bothered us all and breathing became difficult as we struggled on. The minister wanted to stop, but the guide refused. He had to get us all to the top. The mountain was 14,392 feet high!

Crawling up those last thousand feet, which were indeed "the hardest," we finally reached the rim of the crater, the summit, and collapsed in a snow cave carved out by the steam still rising from the crater's depths. The view from the top was spectacular, including the vista of the Pacific to the west. Refreshed by a sandwich and hot tea from a thermos, we were ready to return.

The descent was speedy. Roped to the guide, we slid down the cone's snow banks. Then suddenly he unfastened us and took off down the slopes. Standing upright he skated or glissaded, using his ice axe as a brake, and told us to follow. I knew the danger involved; glissading required practice. I had done it on the Breithorn in Switzerland, where the guide held me by rope from behind. I plunked down in the snow to watch, with the barbers beside me. The minister, however, followed closely behind the guide, who made a sudden right-angle turn and called out a warning. Unable to turn, the minister dropped out of sight. A large crevasse had opened at the head of the glacier. We stomped down the snowy slope, using our ice axes for support while the guide climbed back up. The minister, caught in a great mass of snow that had broken off and fallen with him, was stuck in the crevasse twenty feet below. He had had the wind knocked out, but was conscious. The guide lowered a rope, which the minister was able to tie below his arm pits. Pulling and tugging, we hauled him out, shaky but uninjured. Cautiously we continued on to the hut. After a rest Flo rejoined the group and we made our way back down below tree line to Paradise Inn. I suspect that guide was fired.

My adventure continued south by bus and train down the West Coast to Crater Lake in Oregon. I can still recall standing on the rim and gazing down at the sparkling blue lake below. I found it hard to imagine that here only a few centuries before had stood a majestic mountain (similar to Mount St. Helens before the explosion). The whole top of the summit had simply collapsed, leaving a great hole that filled with water. A side trip to Yosemite National Park and those majestic walls of granite followed.

Several days still remained before the start of the geology camp in Colorado. With careful planning I could visit the Grand Canyon by taking the Santa Fe train from Los Angeles to Flagstaff and a second train to the canyon. With two full days to explore, I hired a mule and decided to take one of the less-traveled paths, Hermit's Trail, and planned to spend the night at a camp in the depths of the canyon. As I descended from the hard, gray, limestone rim at the top of the plateau, the pages of time seemed to turn back. The rocks were different: red colors of shale, buff-colored sandstones. It was hot; I loitered along the way before reaching the camp. Leaving my mule, I climbed down to the bottom of the column, the basement upon which great seas had built those massive walls above. Refreshed by a shower in a small cascade, I returned to Hermit's Rest.

The following day the route led along the Tonto Platform on a narrow shelf of red shale, ending at the junction of the Bright Angel Trail, the customary route used by tourists. Here, I followed my tired mule on foot up the dusty, zigzag trail, which rose in time to rejoin the limestone plateau. That night, sitting on the rim in the evening light, I watched the shadows creep up, cutting out the millions of years that lay hidden below. I was eager to build on this glimpse of the past. The insights and perspective I gained at the Grand Canyon were to be an inspiration for the career that lay ahead.

I arrived in time at the Colorado camp west of Boulder, where I had a chance to see some of the local mining and prospecting pits and to explore that area of the Continental Divide. A short time still remained at the end of the camp course before I had to leave for Wisconsin. But first I wanted to climb Longs Peak, which we had seen on the trips from the Colorado site. I joined a group for the horseback ride through the fir forests to a high point on the mountain. A short climb over the great granite ledges to the summit provided us an unforgettable view of Rocky Mountain National Park spread out below.

I still had time to cram in one more trip before Wisconsin. I chose Dream Lake, which I could explore from the Estes Park Hotel, where I was staying. I hired a horse and set out with blankets and food. The first night I encountered no problem, tethering the horse and sleeping by a stream under the pine and spruce of the virgin forest. Next day, we reached the beautiful little lake in whose waters were reflected the mountains above. The trail passed around the end of the lake beneath the cliffs. The water was high and the trail was flooded, but there was no other way to go. My choice was to continue or to retrace my steps. I coaxed the horse; he wouldn't budge. Then I dismounted, pushed, and threw pebbles at his tail. Still no movement. Since the foot-high water frightened him, I tried tying my bandanna across his eyes as blinders. This did the trick. We finally made our way across.

It was time to go east to Wisconsin. Before heading to Madison to start work, I dashed back to New England by train to see my mother. Traveling by sleeper provided me a good view of the countryside during the day and even a glimpse of Niagara Falls in the middle of the night.

Kay (right) with tent-mates at University of Colorado mountain camp, Summer 1925

Kay with plane table and alidade, Baraboo Ridge, Wisconsin, 1925

Breaking into a Man's World

I N SEPTEMBER 1925 I arrived at the University of Wisconsin, headlong into the breach. Unbeknownst to me, for several years the geology faculty had awarded the single geology-geography fellowship to someone in their department; the geographers had not had an outside applicant assigned to them for some time and were up in arms. To mollify the feuding interests, a compromise was reached: if the geographers voted for the geology fellowship applicant in 1924, the geology department would return the favor in 1925. So when my name came up, the geography committee presented me as their candidate, assuming that since I was a woman, I would be a geographer. The head of the geology department, however, knew that as a student under Miss Bascom at Bryn Mawr, I would be well trained in geology. With tongue firmly planted in cheek, the geologists supported my application. Despite my pleas, I was confronted by the geographers upon my arrival and told I was to be "one of them." So to satisfy their wishes, I had to take a seminar in geography and complete a thesis under their auspices. I was, however, allowed to enroll in a course in physiography. My busy schedule was filled out with a couple of geology courses as well as classes in meteorology and glacial geology, which provided me the chance to gain the background I wanted while proving if I could compete as an equal with men. The University of Wisconsin had never had women in their geology department before.

In the first meeting of the geography seminar, we were instructed to draw a map of the Great Lakes and to mark the main cities. Then we were asked to choose our areas of concentration for our master's theses. The geography professor must have been sadly disappointed with me. I had no idea of how to draw the lakes and could place only Detroit and Chicago on my feeble rendering. How could I do a geography study when I knew no geography? A compromise was struck and I was assigned a paper on the origin of the Great Lakes from physiographic and geologic perspectives. I was to work under Professor Lobeck, whose field of physiography was closely related to geography and whose knowledge I had experienced firsthand on the summer trip out west.

This solution suited me. I was gaining valuable counsel from Professor Lobeck. He taught map reading by using maps from all

University of Wisconsin Lake Superior trip, Spring 1926. Back row, second from left, Professor Mead, Kay, Mickey (Emily Hahn)

over the United States, correlating the physiography as well as the geology of the areas studied. He was also a master of drawing block diagrams as an aid to interpreting a region. This visual method stood me well over the years. One day, when he was unexpectedly called away, he asked me to teach the class in physiography. I was to discuss the Glacier Park region with a group composed entirely of male geologists. Quite a challenge. My solution to this potentially disastrous situation was to present myself as the equal of those who had eyed me with such skepticism when I began. My strategy worked.

The structural geology course I took was made up of the same men. In those days, in the study of structural geology, the theory of "isostasy" was the rule. Accordingly, it was held that the earth moved up and down as mountains were denuded and basins formed. Intrusives were thrust into the region. The professor in charge used to quote a line from the Pick and Hammer Club of Washington D.C., "What makes the earth's stratum bust? Isostasy. Isostasy." Today, the theory is all plate tectonics, according to which great blocks of the earth's crust push back and forth to form mountains and land masses. How the world has changed!

I had apparently made my mark with the men. The group stood by me the next semester when I signed up for the course in Lake Superior geology, which involved a week-long field trip. No female had ever been allowed to go. Professor Mead, who was to run the course, had flatly stated that a woman couldn't make the trip. It was too much of a hardship. The men immediately got busy to see what could be done. In addition to me, they had to fight for an engineering major named Mickey, who was similarly determined to barge into a man's world.

Professor Mead was in a dilemma about how to handle the situation. He would not let us go. He talked it over with the dean of the university, who concurred and referred the matter to the dean of women. When Mickey and I got separate summonses to the dean of women's office, the students decided to take matters into their own hands. Trying to make us look studious, they made me wear a pair of horn-rimmed glasses and lengthened my short skirt and told Mickey to dress conservatively and carry a bundle of books in her arms.

Mickey and I arrived to meet the dean at the same time. She seated us in front of her desk and took out several folders, asking why we were taking the course. My reply was to outline my interest in mining and the necessity of doing fieldwork. Mickey, as an engineering major, said she needed the firsthand experience. The dean studied Mickey's record and found that at least that week, she was not on the dean's "bad" list. Mickey was often in trouble. Then, not finding much about me, she said, "Of course you come from Bryn Mawr, so your record goes without question," and inquired if I would be willing to undertake the responsibility of being the chaperone of the party. I gave a quick look at Mickey, who was trying not to explode with laughter, and replied that I would be happy to. Off we went. The dean then wrote to Professor Mead, expressing her view that I would be an adequate chaperone for the group.

At this point, I must digress and write a word about my friend Mickey, whose real name was Emily Hahn. In time she became a well-known author, gaining fame with tales of her colorful life. Her first book, *Seductio ad absurdum,* was published while she was still in college. She later became a regular writer for the *New Yorker.* Mickey spent several years in China, where she married a Chinese man. In 1937, when the Japanese invaded China, she was able to save her husband's printing press and persuade the Japanese of her Chinese citizenship. Her cleverness saved her from being sent to a concentration camp with the rest of the foreigners. She also managed to visit her lover, Colonel Boxer, with whom she had a baby out of wedlock. When he was captured and jailed for the duration of the Japanese incident, she found a way to supply him with food and luxuries. Eventually she married the colonel in the United States and wrote about these experiences in a book entitled *China to Me.*

Years later, when I was working for a gold-mining company in Africa, Mickey wanted to visit. Since her boat did not stop in Freetown, Sierra Leone, the port of debarkation for our rendezvous, she continued on to the Congo, taking an extensive trip into the heart of Africa. She wrote a book about this journey, *Congo Solo.* I always hoped she might arrive on my doorstep one day and write the story of my life. Instead, at age ninety, I have had to do it myself. What a book she would have made!

With me as chaperone, Professor Mead was stuck with not one but two females. We left in high spirits. At first he was obviously disgruntled, but gradually, his sense of humor returned. In our anxiety not to be burdensome, we set a hard pace. On the first day, as he was puffing along behind Mickey, the professor grabbed her leather jacket, pulled her behind him, and said, "I'll flunk you if you get ahead of me again!"

On the second day of our trip we were introduced to a well-known geologist, who was taking us to some outcrops. Smoking a cigar, he said to Mickey, "You can't become an engineer if you don't smoke." Mickey promptly grabbed his stogie and smoked it to the end. She looked quite green. All her life she did outrageous things. And she even smoked cigars in her later years!

On the third day we were to go into an iron mine. We lined up and Professor Mead, whose sense of humor and acceptance of our presence was established, said to the foreman, "Jim. I'd like to introduce you to the group this year. First," he said turning to me, "here is the chaperone." Then, gesturing toward Mickey, "And this is the engineer of the party. The others are the geologists." We had made our place in their world.

Years later, when Professor Mead was head of the geology department at MIT and we would meet at an occasional dinner party, he delighted in regaling the diners with the tale of how he had been duped into taking me along. I, in turn, recalled how valuable the trip had been when I later found myself studying iron ores in West Africa. I could never have faced the problems there without that Lake Superior experience.

Another crucial class for me was the spring vacation mapping course at Baraboo, Wisconsin. Again, I was the first woman to enroll along with another, Muck, who was engaged to a young geologist working in Indonesia. We were warned about the hardships and

Mapping instruction, University of Wisconsin, 1925. Kay (left) and Muck (second from right)

lodged at a farmhouse rather than with the men, who had to stay in a barn-like dormitory.

The first day Muck and I were presented with a plane table and an alidade and assigned to make a map of the Baraboo Ridge. We had already been taught how to use these instruments at the university. Off we set shortly after seven in the morning. Before long we found that we could not possibly finish the task by five, the time we were supposed to return. Undaunted, we continued along the ridge until sunset, when we found ourselves at the top. We still had to get sightings down to the railroad to finish our traverse. I sent Muck down to the railroad over the scree with the plane table, while I waited for her to shout "OK." It was quite dark by the time I got her signal, a white handkerchief waving. I set the alidade by her voice and the white rag. Carefully, I crawled down to the railroad over the slippery talus. We still had a long walk to get back to base camp. When we arrived, we were met by a frantic professor and a roomful of anxious young men. The professor learned his lesson about stubborn females. We discovered that he had no intention of our being able to complete the traverse. It was just a test to reveal our incapacity for finishing a project. After that he gave us very short assignments for fear we would really become benighted in our anxiety to prove our mettle.

The 'Laidy' Geologist

AS WAS MY WONT, I had planned a full summer after classes ended and left the University of Wisconsin early, before graduation. A friend in the biology department said she would impersonate me and pick up my diploma. Off I headed by train to the Black Hills of South Dakota, a place where the whole sequence of geologic history is exposed. The central section contains the oldest rocks, while successive layers of the time period are revealed along the flanks of the interior. The train stopped at the southern edge of the hills, where I checked my large duffel bag. With a knapsack and the minimum of clothes for two weeks, I set off on foot, hitchhiking across the central mass to the Homestake Gold Mine, examining the outcrops as I walked. I was lucky to get an occasional lift from a passing motorist or wagon.

The scenery in the Black Hills was magnificent. High spires of "needles" carved by erosion, sculpted by wind and rain, were found in the central highlands, untouched by glaciation. I came upon Spearfish Canyon, cut deep in the limestone of the lowlands. I hiked a mile and a half to the bottom of the gorge to explore, finally reaching the Homestake Gold Mine far in the interior. Here, at Susie's Boarding House, I met a group of student engineers from the University of Wisconsin. Their professor agreed to allow me to accompany them underground the following day. The miners were superstitious of women going underground. But disguised as one of the boys, I would not be noticed. Word got around that a female was in the party. They picked out an engineer who was much shorter than I and decided that he was the one. He never forgave me.

After the trip underground, I accompanied the engineers through the large stamp mill, built in a series of steps down into a canyon. Gravity took the crushed rock from the top of the mill down to the lowest level. Every eleven days the gold was recovered from the long process of removing it by crushing the rock and sorting it. I was fortunate to be there on the day that four red-hot bricks of molten gold worth $100,000 apiece were recovered in the final process. Guards with six-shooters stood around. The bricks were taken in a secure car and shipped immediately to New York by train.

After leaving the Homestake Mine, I headed east to a geology camp run by the University of Missouri where I spent two interesting days studying the sequence of upturned beds, which showed the successive periods of submergence of the central United States. Then I headed back toward the railroad with plans to reach Glacier Park in about ten days to join a field trip run by Northwestern University.

Time was running out. The first day I was lucky to get a lift in the back of a logging truck. When I got off the driver looked at me and said, "Oh! If I had known you were a woman, I would have had you up front." At first glance, with my knapsack, brown canvas hat, bandanna, leather jacket, dungarees, and hobnailed boots, I passed as a boy. But this was almost my undoing. The next car to come along was a tumbledown Model T Ford with two rather rough-looking men who said they were going as far as Custer. This would get me well on my way. I began to get a bit nervous, however, when I got rather knowing sidelong glances. I tried to answer their questions as ambiguously as possible. Eventually, one of the men got out near his cabin. The driver continued on past Custer, saying that he would put me up for the night. Alarmed, I saw no way to escape. Finally, he drew up to a log cabin three miles out of town and showed me in. He pointed to the bunk where we would sleep that night. How was I to extricate myself from this mess? My mind was racing in circles. A gun in the corner didn't look too promising if I tried to escape. Sensing by then that he had obviously seen through my "boy" disguise, I was desperate. When he finally went to the outhouse, I simply picked up my knapsack and ran as fast as I could up his drive and into the hills beyond. I didn't stop until I was hidden in the scrub quite far from the cabin. I wasn't sure whether he would try to hunt for me but I was taking no chances and waited until it was almost dark. Then I worked my way down to the road and walked the three miles back into Custer, where I stayed the night in a small hotel. Having had enough of hitchhiking, I took the bus back to the railroad station the next day and bought a ticket to Butte, Montana, where I hoped to visit the copper mines before heading north to Glacier Park.

At the hotel in Butte I ran into Professor Mead, who was doing some geological work for the mining company. Hearing of my wish to go underground, he very kindly promised to arrange it. The next day he sent his own special helper, Jim, a very knowledgeable Irish miner, to guide me. Arriving at the main shaft, I was outfitted with hard hat and heavy overalls. We descended 2,000 feet in a cage and then proceeded by foot through many tunnels. Jim knew all the best places for showing me the ore. At one point I was having some difficulty descending from one level to the next. As I was climbing down a ladder on an "exploring" trip, a miner called from below, "Hey, there, young fella. You'll never get down that way. Put your left foot first till you feel the rung." Feeling proud of his charge, Jim called down, "That ain't no young fella. That's a 'laidy' geologist." I got many stares. But with these words I had finally gained the recognition I had worked so hard to attain.

That night, Professor Mead invited me to dinner. When he found out I was planning to hitchhike north to Glacier Park, he threw a fit. But I was adamant. I was due there in four days. Later that evening there was a knock on my door. The hotel manager had come to say he had found an army officer going to Missoula who had agreed to give me a lift. We left bright and early the next day. That afternoon he dropped me at a small boardinghouse in Missoula, Montana. Later that evening he called to say there was a private going to Glacier Park the next day who would be glad to drive me. All was arranged and I reached my destination without further incident and in plenty of time to meet the group.

Narrow Escape

THE SUMMER field course offered by Northwestern University in Glacier National Park, Montana, was run by a woman geologist, Peggy Fuller, who was making a geological map of the region. I never knew whether the class was "for women only," but Peggy arrived with four women seniors, all majoring in geology. One eventually married a geologist; none went on to become geologists, except me.

We were based in a small town at the foot of Lake McDonald. We worked out from there, taking buses to distant areas or hiking in that section. At the end of three weeks, we were given separate projects. The four girls paired up, leaving me to work alone on my assignment — to find and study any outcrops along the southwestern shore of Lake McDonald. I started out shortly after seven in the morning. Skirting the shore, I found nothing until I reached a small point about a mile north of the town. I then decided to go inland for a quarter of a mile to higher ground. I made a traverse north, then planned to return to the lakeshore and head back. It was a hot day, with air thick with smoke from forest fires to the west of the park. The forest of virgin pines had very little underbrush, which made the going easy. While eating a late lunch, half asleep and gazing through the treetops, I was suddenly startled to find cinders dropping around me. Some were red-hot. The smoke had thickened and I began to feel drowsy. But I came to life in a hurry when I saw and heard flames in the trees above. As I scrambled to my feet, a rainstorm of glowing cinders fell around me. I took off full tilt for the lake.

The fire was spreading across the treetops. A couple of deer and some rabbits dashed madly along with me, heading for water. I put on my leather jacket as protection from the sparks and pulled my hat down low. The smoke and sudden warmth of the flames spreading in the brush made me panic. Gasping, I reached a small cabin on the lakeshore and took shelter down wind behind it. Everything seemed to be on fire. I could tell that the cabin would soon be consumed too. Heading south over the rocky banks of the lake, I tried to keep out of the timber, which grew right down to the lakeshore. At last, reaching the projecting outcrops I had studied that morning, I looked down toward the cove, which lay above the town. I found my way cut off; the fire was already ahead of me.

All I could do was sit tight in the lee of the rocks. I kept my jacket wet by sprinkling water on it and tied my wet bandanna across my face to help my breathing. I had noticed a few motorboats on the lake, but was unable to attract their attention. They were keeping well away from the flames. As dark was approaching, I decided I would have to sit it out in my uncomfortable shelter. Strange to say, I was getting cold, even with all that fire around me. I dragged a few nearby branches to the rock and made a little fire of my own.

I had almost given up hope of rescue when I heard another motorboat, idling along, a little nearer than the others. I knew they must be looking for me. It came close and then started to turn back. I tied my red bandanna on a stick and waved it frantically, but they couldn't hear my shouting over the crackle of bursting branches. Suddenly the boat turned toward me. I had been seen! They did not dare to come in too close to the flames and called to me when they were as near as they could get. I would have to swim out to them. Without thinking, I jumped in, hammer and notebook around my waist, knapsack on my back. I should have removed my heavy hobnailed boots. I was weak from inhaling smoke and almost sank before reaching the helping hands that hauled me aboard. They immediately gunned the boat to get away from the fire.

Peggy, our instructor, was in the boat, hysterical. No one would believe her when she had told them that one of her students was at the lake, caught in the conflagration. Fortunately, she had run into the same forest ranger to whom she had introduced all of us in the early part of our stay. He was quite alarmed and commandeered a motorboat from one of the cottages on the lake. They had searched several times without success. As darkness was approaching, Peggy persuaded them to take one final look. Luckily, she spotted my bandanna just before they had given up.

By the time we got back, the town had been evacuated. The girls had packed up my things with theirs and then departed for the railroad station. When I arrived there, my friends dug out some dry clothes for me. I was feeling much better by the time the train came and took us to the Glacier Park Hotel at the east entrance. I must admit that I had a sleepless night; I kept having nightmares of being consumed by flames.

Apparently, some reporters had interviewed the group at the hotel. They must have seen me with my close-cropped hair, looking rather bedraggled. The next day, in the August 2, 1926, edition of the *Great Falls Tribune,* it was reported that "a girl was caught in the fire … and waded up to her ears in the lake to escape. Holding a handkerchief aloft on a stick she signalled for help and finally was rescued." It was later discovered that the fire had been caused by the exploding gasoline tank of an old Model T Ford as it reached the rise of land not too far above the place where I had been dozing. The strong west wind had quickly spread the flames, consuming a whole section of the park on the west side of Lake McDonald.

I stayed on in the park after the course was over and took a pack trip north to the Waterton Lakes on the Canadian border, where I found more information for Peggy's map, much to her delight.

Too soon it was time to return east to see my family before continuing with my studies. I had decided to enter Columbia University to work toward a doctorate in geology and I was eager to begin.

Kay (left) and Marie Devon Hendricks take an early dip and enjoy a snowball fight, Wyoming camp, Summer 1927

Doctoral Pursuits

COLUMBIA HAD BEEN highly recommended. Not only were there several outstanding professors in my field of interest, but they were supportive of women preparing for careers in the sciences. Columbia University is on Morningside Heights, a part of New York City that in those days had more open space than the downtown area. It did not seem as confined as the city itself. The air was pure and there were trees on the campus. I took a room in the women's graduate dorm, which was a short walk to my classes. The geology department had three women students. Space was limited and we were all assigned tables in the library for studying. Across the hall was a good mineral collection and the basement housed the fossils. We spent many hours poring through the cases of drawers. In our spare time we hung out in an extra space in the basement that we called the "Dinosaur Club," which opened to the entrance area above. One could always look down to see who was there. I admit to dropping a paper bag "bomb" full of water on a group one afternoon, breaking up an intense discussion that I felt needed an injection of humor and laughter. We were all working too hard and needed a little levity.

At this time Mother was living in New Hampshire in the house where I was born, having left Plymouth Street while I was in college. First she had moved to North Andover to be with her unmarried sister in Gramma's house. This arrangement did not work out, as Aunt Harriet was much too set in her ways. Then Mother decided to winterize the beach house and travel to warmer climates in the coldest months. On Christmas vacation that year I visited my mother in Bermuda. It was cold and raw. Since swimming was out of the question, I bicycled around the island. The semi-tropical countryside was a pleasant change from the crowded city streets of New York. It was a refreshing holiday.

Columbia offered a summer field course in conjunction with the University of Wyoming that met high in the Medicine Bow Mountains, where a large cabin and tent sites had been built to house the students. "Doc" Knight, the only professor of geology at

the university, ran the camp most efficiently. I signed up for the
course, determined to do some field study in the West and hoping to
find a subject for my thesis. Also enrolled were two of the men in the
Columbia geology group. We went west from New York by sleeper in
early June, accompanied by Professor Berkey, my advisor and head
of the geology department at Columbia. My birthday happened to
fall on the second day of travel and I was presented with a dozen red
roses from a Columbia admirer. They had been secreted in the refrig-
erator of the dining car.

The next morning, as we descended from the train in Laramie,
Wyoming, we were met by Doc and the whole student group. I was
never so embarrassed in my life as when I climbed down from the
train carrying that bunch of red roses. We had all become quite ill in
the night from food poisoning in the creamed chicken. We must
have looked like a funeral procession. Professor Berkey went directly
to the hospital while the rest of us were driven to the camp in old
Franklin cars and promptly put to bed in our tents, which were scattered around the unsightly wooden main building that was to be our
meeting quarters, dining room, and kitchen. There we were at 8,000
feet in the Medicine Bow Mountains, surrounded by beautiful fir
trees. Snow still covered the ground.

My tent-mate, Marie, turned out to be one of the women who had
been with my group in Glacier Park. Since I had recovered by the
next morning, Marie and I decided to take a quick dip in the icy
brook near our tent. Some of the boys got wind of this and when we
came out of the frigid stream, they pelted us with snowballs. We were
told later that we had bathed in their drinking water.

The course began with three strenuous weeks of trips to the
heights to study the rocks. We even climbed 12,000 feet to the summit of Medicine Bow Peak. We also had excursions down to the valleys to get acquainted with the more recent sediments of the region.
Doc always gave us a lecture at night, illustrating his talks with crayon
drawings on a blackboard he had set up, skillfully drawing the structures of the regions we would visit the next day.

The highlight of the trip was camping out in Plumbago Canyon in
the Laramie Mountains. Doc's three special helpers and the drivers
of the Franklin cars got up at dawn. We could hear their pistol shots
as they went about shooting rattlesnakes, at least a dozen of which
were sunning themselves on the rocks. It was then safe for us to
explore the variegated formations later in the day. All morning our
short, plump chaperone dogged Doc's footsteps. She was taking no

Roadside camp with Franklin cars, University of Wyoming trip, Summer 1927

chances of stepping on a snake. The rocks and the granite-like intrusions called anorthosites that had invaded them caught my interest. I decided on the spot that these would be the subject of my thesis. My decision later met the approval of Professor Berkey when he returned to camp from the hospital.

At the close of the first three weeks' session, Doc offered the students a trip to the Grand Canyon, Zion National Park, and Bryce Canyon National Park. Needless to say, I signed up. We loaded our sleeping rolls on the running boards or outside bumpers of the Franklin cars and took along "tepee" tents, which slept two. A truck driven by Doc contained the provisions for the trip. The two Columbia students and I had brought along William Morris Davis's physiography text and the German translation to prepare for the German exams the next year. Whenever one of the Franklins broke down or had a flat, which was often, we would get out Davis's book, sit in the shade of one of the cars, and take turns reading the German edition while one of us held the English text. This saved having a dictionary along. We all passed our German exams that next spring.

One hazard of driving in those days before safety glass was that passing trucks or cars would throw a stone against our windscreens, shattering them. Since most of the roads were gravel, this was a common occurrence. When we drove up for gas, we always got a kick out of the gas station attendants, who would look for the radiator to add water. Franklins had neither radiators nor cooling systems.

Kay (far right) at north rim of the Grand Canyon with University of Wyoming group, 1927

Arriving at the Grand Canyon, we camped on the north rim. Doc's diagrams were an invaluable help in interpreting the millions of years that it had taken to build up the layers of sediments. Next we drove on to camp below the high granite cliffs of Zion National Park and continued to Bryce Canyon with its thousands of colorful spires sculpted from the soft sediments. Even now, I know of no better way to study geology.

Driving along on our return in the Franklin cars, with their tops down, we leaned back, our legs hanging out over the packed duffel bags. We counted the cottontail rabbits for amusement as we rolled along toward Salt Lake City and headed back toward Wyoming. On our last day, as we were crossing the desert-like Wyoming flatlands, we stopped, as usual, for a quick roadside lunch. Doc opened the "chuck wagon" and began handing out large tins of what he hoped were pineapple slices. The labels had washed off. We opened one can after another. Our last meal, as we perspired in the blazing sun, was chili con carne!

Anxious to avoid the hay fever season in the East, I stayed on at the camp until I had to return to Columbia in the fall. Since the camp cook had departed, Doc asked me to take over food preparation for the dozen or so people remaining. I did not admit I had never really cooked anything since my failure to put yeast in my bread at the Winsor School. I hate to think of the awful meals I put on the table: mostly canned baked beans and carrots as entrée, marshmallow on graham crackers for dessert.

Back at Columbia, I completed a year of thesis preparation and study for the orals, the final hurdle to qualify for thesis work. They had finally caught up with me, I thought. I would be questioned by all the professors of the geology department, each of whom would have a half hour to examine me. I was sure the man from paleontology was "out to get me"; he was known to dislike women in geology.

The night before my exam I stayed up until three in the morning going through all of the boxes of fossils in the basement. At midnight who should walk into the stacks but the paleontology professor. "What! You didn't go to Einstein's lecture?" he asked in amazement. He had just come back, and here I was, cramming on fossils. The next day at the exam in the large lecture hall, crowded with all my friends, he asked me to discuss Einstein's theory. I mumbled something about infinity. My friends were horror-stricken.

The mineralogy professor, on the other hand, had a sense of humor. He always came with a tray of minerals for identification, which reputedly included a wild card. When I picked up a green specimen, I immediately knew "this was it." I said it resembled green quartz from the top of Medicine Bow Mountain. I was right. In spite of the paleontology professor, I managed to pass.

Mapping the Laramies

I HAD SPENT a good deal of time at Columbia preparing myself for my fieldwork the next summer in the Laramie Mountains of Wyoming. In early June 1928 I was ready to set out. In need of a car for transportation, I finally gave in and bought an old Model A Ford for $250. With my new driver's license I set out from New York City with a friend and headed for Massachusetts to collect my gear and say good-bye to my mother, who was dubious about the safety of my working alone in "that wilderness." Professor Berkey was equally horrified when he learned that I was going to work solo. But there was no one available to accompany me and I was quite confident that there would be no problems.

On the way to Boston, one by one the tires of the old Ford blew out. With no money to buy new ones, we had to stop at garages along the way for patches. Even the spare was no good. We didn't make it to Boston that day. Finally, exhausted, we stopped after midnight at a roominghouse. Needless to say, my mother treated me to four new tires so I could make the trip out west.

Setting out again I picked up Baldie, a college friend, who met me in Albany. She was headed for the West Coast and thought the trip together would be fun. Just outside of Ames, Iowa, while Baldie was driving, the car skidded on the fresh gravel that had recently been poured on the road. It had not yet packed down. We spun over into the ditch and into a fence, unhurt, but with much damage to the car. Those old Fords could be put together by patching them here and there and in two days, with much rattling and squeaking, we resumed our journey. Baldie refused to drive again.

After bidding good-bye to Baldie in Laramie, I loaded up with enough food for ten days and took off. The Laramie Mountains were wide open ranges. Sheep roamed the upland area, driven by a sheep-herder from the large King Ranch. He lived in a covered wagon, which was moved about as the sheep grazed areas within a five-mile radius. As a result of overgrazing, a mass of sagebrush was all that remained when the sheep moved on. Wild horses were also foraging about, north of the sheep areas, where the fodder was still plentiful. They were occasionally rounded up and taken down to the railroad to be sent to Chicago for slaughter. Cattle wandered about in herds. I never saw anyone caring for them. At least *they* didn't destroy the soil.

Kay practicing rattlesnake shooting, Summer 1928

Scattered around the borders of the mountain mass were a few homesteaders, who made pathetic little gardens in the gullies. In general, the country was wild, open range with very few trees, except in the small gulches. The area where the anorthosites were found was about forty miles long and ten miles wide. A few dirt tracks came up from the lowlands for access to the height of land, which rose

Rocksie with the Ford on the Laramie Mountains upland, 1928

1,000 feet above the plains. I had to negotiate these slopes to get to the anorthosites, which made up the whole central part of the region. My plan was to locate at the head of the gullies, leave my car and tepee tent, and work out by foot as far as I could wander. Then I would move on to the next gully. In this way, I could cover the whole region, which I figured would take me about three months.

The anorthosites had a bluish-gray color, contrasting with the pink of the granite, which had intruded into this large body at a later date. Since the feldspars that made up the two types of rock were different, it was easy to distinguish them. Because the Laramies had not been glaciated, it was often difficult to find outcrops in the weathered soil, except in the gullies or wind-blown uplands. My first attempt to reach the higher ground was frustrating. The Ford just couldn't make the grade up a steep hill. Then I got the bright idea of going up backward. This worked.

Starting out, I set up my tepee tent in a depression where the dirt road ran out. Here I worked for a week, covering as much distance as feasible from this first camp. Water was a problem. I had come with only two canvas bags filled with drinking water, which I hung over the side of the Ford. I was able to get some water for washing in the gully nearby. Scouting possible routes over dirt tracks to move camp, I covered the higher ground in the south fairly quickly. Since the sheep had overgrazed this area, outcrops could be easily seen.

When my food ran out, I returned to Laramie and stayed in the small hotel to bathe and wash my clothes. The university campus cafeteria was nearby, where I could have some real meals. Several stray dogs were casing the cafeteria for handouts. One sad-looking sheep dog attached himself to me. He was obviously lost. The students said he had been around for some time. I decided to adopt him and named him Rocksie. Loading up with dog food and some fresh vegetables to supplement my canned goods, I took off again. First, I had to stop at a brook to give Rocksie a scrubbing. The dog turned out to be a good companion and took to my outdoor life as if he had always lived on the range.

Week after week I repeated this pattern. Early in September I had a short visit from a friend from Bryn Mawr. It was good to have someone to talk to. She was most helpful in building a makeshift bridge of logs and boards to cross a swampy area to reach one of my distant working points. Four hands were better than two.

One evening, when I had returned from bringing fresh supplies from town, I took pity on an old sheepherder who ran his flock where I was working. Inviting him for supper, I served a tuna fish salad with the fresh vegetables I had bought and a dessert of fruit. He thanked me, adding that he guessed he liked his baked beans better than my "fancy" food. A few of the homesteaders through whose lands I roamed were rather suspicious of my actions. I am sure they watched me from afar. Others were shy and friendly. One family at the north end of my area of study let me set up my tepee tent along their brook. They sent out one of their boys with some fresh cake for my supper and even invited me for a wonderful home-cooked meal the last night of my stay there.

One night I was camped along a tiny brook on the uplands. Since it was a beautiful evening, I didn't pitch my tent but chose instead to sleep in my bedroll beside the water. Fortunately, I had put Rocksie in the Ford. In the middle of the night I woke to the sound of hoof-beats all around. A herd of wild horses was snuffling and whinnying. I froze in place. Fortunately, they didn't trample me.

Another adventure involved my coming upon a group of six men holed up in an abandoned prospect pit cut in the hillside. Right off, I sensed trouble. They were obviously bootleggers making whiskey of some sort (Prohibition was still the law of the land) and I had stumbled upon their hideout. I eyed their rifles, lined up along the wall, and decided to "play dumb." They gloomily listened to me talk with great enthusiasm about my studies. I commented about their having found a quiet place to set up camp, remarking that I had not run into much game in the area, only rabbits, a fox, and a few grouse. Not a word from them. I wished them good hunting and departed. I don't know if they believed that I didn't suspect what they were up to. I had left my car hidden along the road while I wandered off into the uplands. When I returned, an armed man jumped out from behind, gave me one look, and apologized for the scare. He was the sheriff out looking for moonshiners. He had been told there was a suspicious person roaming the hills. His day-long wait was not rewarded. I was able, however, to alert him to the men in the prospect pit. I certainly was glad to be finished in that area.

Near the railroad to the extreme south, a few two-story wooden houses had sprung up. The occupants simply disappeared when I was looking for outcrops in that area. Rumor had it that there were moonshiners hidden away in some of the buildings. Once in a while I would glance up and see a curtain move. They were watching.

On a small hill called Iron Mountain was a large deposit of iron ore at the southeastern edge of the anorthosite mass; I spent several days studying its occurrence. The weather was fine, so I took my bedroll to a place near the base of the outcrops in order to save time. One evening a sudden thunderstorm came up just as I was going to sleep. The lightning was attracted to the iron and flashes were hitting all around. I had seen patches of fused rock where there had been previous strikes. I lay there, knowing that I was safe inside my blankets. It was eerie to have my hair stand on end. You can be sure I slept in the tent near my car the following nights.

In this area the thunderstorms would come up without warning. Rain-slicked roads were also a problem; it was easy to get stuck and safer to wait until they dried. One day, when I was returning to Laramie, a sudden shower turned the road into red mud. I skidded into the ditch. A few hours later, a farmer came along with his wagon and obligingly hauled me back on to the now dried road.

At one point during my trip, Doc Knight brought the field group to Plumbago Canyon, where I joined them. I had the chance to discuss the progress of my work with him and also seized the opportunity to get many samples of the Plumbago rocks to study under the microscope the next winter. I had been leery of going near this rattlesnake den area alone. Because the men had cleared out or scared away the rattlers in their early morning shooting sally, this was a great time for me to work without fear. Although I had purchased a 32 Colt automatic and been given target practice by the men, I never bothered to carry the pistol with me. I had too much equipment with my hammer, compass, barometer, map, and writing case tied around my waist. I also had a knapsack on my back for my lunch and specimens. I am sure I could never have hit a rattler, anyway.

By mid-September I was ready to return east. I decided to take Rocksie with me; no one wanted him in Laramie. Fortunately, I found a home for him with elderly relatives with a Scottish chauffeur, who immediately adopted him. Rocksie must have reminded him of the sheep dogs back home.

I worked hard all winter, studying thin sections of the rocks I had collected. To complete the doctoral requirements, I had to organize my thesis into a paper that would be accepted by the *American Journal of Science*. At Columbia at this time, work had to be published in the form in which it was submitted. I also had to pass the oral exam. All went well.

With this behind me, I was free to decide what to do with my life. Heretofore I had strenuously avoided getting involved with anyone or anything that might interfere with my getting my degree. I had seen too many classmates give up their ambitions for marriage. I had decided that was not going to happen to me.

PART II

Prospecting in West Africa and Other Adventures

Kay on geology congress trip, South Africa, 1929

A Fateful Decision

IRST I HAD to see the world. My starting point was a geological congress being held in Africa that summer of 1929. From there I would begin my adventures, which I had not revealed to anyone. I had to be assured that my Ph.D. was under my belt before I could begin. My mother had died the previous year and left me enough funds for such an escapade. I would look for a job upon my return to the United States.

As it turned out, Professor Berkey was also planning to attend the African congress. I did not want him feeling responsible for me, so I took passage to England and then to Cape Town on the boat ahead of him. He was quite surprised to find me there when he arrived and never understood why I hadn't told him I was going.

In those days the trip to South Africa from Plymouth, England, was a pleasant three weeks' voyage. We spent hours lounging on deck. One morning, while I was reading Gertrude Bell's *Travels in Arabia,* a rather pompous, stern-faced man known as Colonel Jack spotted the title and remarked that I was the only one on board not engrossed in *All Quiet on the Western Front,* which had just been released. Colonel Jack had recently retired from many years in India. Surprisingly, we became good friends. He regaled me with tales of his exploits and I entertained him and others with my antics.

On board I had the reputation of being a light-headed tomboy. One day at lunch I announced to the captain that I needed exercise and wanted to climb to the crow's nest. He dismissed this as a silly American joke. On Sunday, while he was conducting the church service in the lounge, I found my way to the lower deck. Seeing no one nearby, I ascended the iron ladder to the top, startling the sailor on watch. At lunch, I announced to my tablemates that I hadn't been able to see land from atop the crow's nest. The captain almost choked on his food! He was angry but what could he say? After all, I had warned him. I had made several such climbs on Atlantic crossings before but the ladders were always enclosed in funnels. This outdoor setup was much more exciting. Indeed, it was easier than scaling the long fire escape outside my Bryn Mawr dormitory.

The young men at my table envied my nerve. A serious young "don" from Cambridge celebrated the event with a poem that concluded, "If the ship sank, I'd come floating up still a 'buoy.'" Another young man decided we should play a trick on the captain by exchanging clothes for dinner. He dressed in my flowing chiffon evening gown, I wore his tuxedo. All through the meal the captain failed to recognize the "switch." I am not sure he appreciated the joke when he finally noticed what we had done.

At the end of the voyage the sight of Cape Town, with the clouds capping Table Mountain, was welcome indeed. It was here I was to join the members of the geological congress. Since this was the start of my journey through Africa, I had signed up for as many trips as possible. The first traversed the scenic highway around the peninsula to the Cape of Good Hope. With the waves breaking against the cliffs, the view of the mountains rising from the edge of the sea was spectacular. The lovely beaches near the town itself were tempting, but I was shocked to read the signs: "Whites only." Segregation was everywhere: special buses, special lavatories. This was my introduction to apartheid.

A second excursion was to the summit of Table Mountain. Construction was under way on a cable car that would be able to whisk people 3,000 feet up from Cape Town; fifty years later I rode it to the top. The first time, however, we had to climb up a rough and steep trail. One of the members of the climbing party was a young Scot from Edinburgh named Jock Lunn, who was working for the colonial government of England, mapping the boundary between Angola and Rhodesia. Before embarking on my trip, I had written to Sid, one of the Columbia University graduate students who was doing geology for the Bancroft Exploration Company in Northern Rhodesia (Zambia), telling him of my plans to attend the congress and visit his camp, if possible. Coincidentally, he and Jock had met and Sid had shown him pictures from Columbia, pointing out my photo. My introduction to Jock occurred at a difficult spot on the trail. Jock tried to give me a hand but I refused his help. He turned to a friend and remarked, "Whew! What an independent woman!"

As the trips progressed to other places in South Africa, Jock and I found ourselves on the same excursions. We soon became close friends, sharing similar interests. He had obtained his Ph.D. in geology in Edinburgh, where his studies had paralleled my own. We came to enjoy one another's company. Together, we explored underground workings in the gold mines of Johannesburg and ventured into the diamond mines. Although Jock was eight years older than I and well established in his profession, he treated me as an equal and soon decided I was the woman he wanted to marry. By the time we reached Pretoria, Jock had proposed. With this sudden and unexpected pronouncement, I was faced with the decision of my life, one that would direct my whole future. But I had chosen a career and vowed nothing was going to interfere with my plans. Jock knew how important my work was to me and said we could travel and pursue our research together.

I was confused and had no one to consult. My family and friends were on the other side of the ocean. My older brother had long before instilled in me the idea that no one would marry me; I was too plain. But here I was in the south of Africa in love with a man who cared for me. All my contacts with other male geologists had been platonic. This was different. Jock was more of a father figure than the younger men I had been with. He pressed me for an answer.

Finally, I decided to accept Jock's proposal. We planned our wedding for London in late December. By then Jock would be through his job and due a leave. In the meantime I would continue up through Africa, visit areas around the Mediterranean, and then head for England.

Jock went north with me as far as his camp in Northern Rhodesia (Zambia). Victoria Falls was the highlight of the stops as we traveled north with the congress members. The falls lie in Southern Rhodesia (Zimbabwe) and Northern Rhodesia. What a beautiful sight it was in the early morning with the mist rising above the narrow gorge and the roaring of the water as it dropped over cliffs into the canyon. Jock had a friend with a small biplane for sightseeing whom he persuaded to fly me over. From this vantage point I could see the zigzag of the bedrock into which the falls dropped abruptly from the wide river valley above to the vast tropical forest below.

After the falls, Jock and I left the geologists and hunted up Sid's camp, where he was doing traverses. Sid was more than delighted to see us. We kept our wedding plans quiet and he didn't guess our secret. That evening, after supper, he suggested we go out to hunt for game to replenish his food supply. With Sid's assistant Jock went in one direction while Sid and I set out around a "dembo" or swamp-like area, where we hoped to find some game. We soon sighted a beautiful waterbuck, its horns raised high, poised silent and alert. Sid took a shot and to my delight he missed. Sid was flustered but explained his failure. He was nervous because what he really wanted to do was propose marriage to me. I was completely taken aback. Sid had been one of my many male friends at Columbia. I had no inkling that any of them considered me more than just another pal. It fell to me to disillusion Sid with the news of my engagement to Jock. Sid was crestfallen but man enough to congratulate us. He remained a lifelong friend.

After the visit with Sid, I rejoined the congress group in Elisabethville (Lubumbashi), the capital of that part of the Congo (Zaire). We were able to view the uranium mines, seeing some of the well-guarded secret places that were proving so rich for the Belgians. But everywhere we went, I found myself missing Jock and wishing he were at my side.

Caught in the 'Sudd'

W ITH THE END of the congress trips I planned to work my way north through Tanganyika (Tanzania), Kenya, Uganda, and down the Nile to Cairo. Two of the congress members had also planned the same route, so we joined forces. They couldn't do anything else; they were stuck with me. One, a Belgian, was a taciturn mineralogist whom I secretly dubbed "Old Misery." The other was chief geologist for England in the Sudan headed for his boat on the Nile. A middle-aged bachelor, set in his ways, he repeated the same jokes over and over, expecting us to laugh each time. I called him "Stuffy."

It turned out to be a rather awkward situation. Stuffy had told friends that he would be engaged to me by the time we reached the Sudan. He even wrote to the men who were caring for his home in Khartoum to prepare the house for his "bride-to-be." What a pickle I was in. It took him some time to digest the news of my plans, but he was the perfect gentleman. Later, he sent me a wedding present from Cairo, a lovely brass tray inlaid with copper and silver.

The trip through Africa took many weeks as it was necessary to travel by boat or train from one country to another. From Elisabethville in the Belgian Congo we went by paddleboat north down the Luapula (Lualaba) River, one of the large tributary streams that lead into the huge Congo River, delivering mail to small settlements along the waterway. Then the three of us continued by rail to a boat to cross Lake Tanganyika. Here we visited Ujiji, where we shook hands, just as Livingstone and Stanley had done at their historic meeting in 1871.

We continued north by train to Lake Victoria, making stops to see geological formations on the way through Kenya. At last we reached Lake Victoria. We had now come half way from Cape Town to Cairo. Lake Victoria, located on the equator in the very middle of Africa, is the source of the Nile, 3,000 miles south of Cairo. We proceeded to follow the river's course as we journeyed north.

On its route the Nile flows into Lake Albert. We planned to trek a hundred miles north of the lake along its swampy banks to reach its navigable head at Jinga, where we would take a three weeks' boat trip of a thousand miles through the "sudd," the swampy areas of the

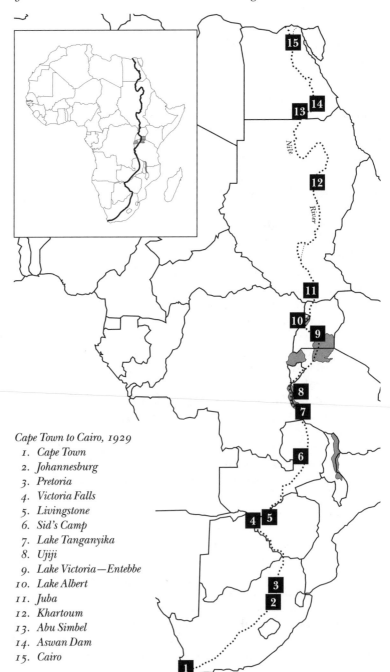

Cape Town to Cairo, 1929
  1. Cape Town
  2. Johannesburg
  3. Pretoria
  4. Victoria Falls
  5. Livingstone
  6. Sid's Camp
  7. Lake Tanganyika
  8. Ujiji
  9. Lake Victoria—Entebbe
  10. Lake Albert
  11. Juba
  12. Khartoum
  13. Abu Simbel
  14. Aswan Dam
  15. Cairo

Map of contemporary Africa by Melissa Mecca

Sudan, before reaching Khartoum, the capital. At Khartoum there was to be a long detour by train around the cataracts of the Nile, then another boat trip before we would reach the Aswan Dam, which was then being built to control the river's floods. The area between Aswan and Cairo is one of Egypt's richest agricultural areas. North of Cairo, the Nile had formed an enormous delta, two hundred miles long as its waters reached the Mediterranean at its mouth.

We began our expedition by boarding a small steamship at Lake Victoria for a three days' trip to Uganda. At Entebbe, the capital, we traveled by car to see the headwaters of the Nile. Graceful fish could be seen leaping high in the rushing waters of the cascade. Hippopotamuses grazed lazily, half submerged in the swamp below the falls. From the source of the Nile we went north by boat and lorry to reach Lake Albert. It was here that I noticed my duffel bag looked awfully flat. To my chagrin, my army cot had been stolen. I had nothing to sleep on at overnight stops. The chief of the village where we stayed the first night presented me with a cot made of strips of skin stretched across a frame. My sleeping comfort was assured. The second night of our detour, the local district commissioner (D.C.) invited me to stay in his house. Instinct told me he couldn't be trusted. I elected to sleep in a hammock strung between the rafters of the small rest house where Old Misery and Stuffy were staying. Their privacy would be invaded. I am sure they resented my turning down the offer of a good bed.

Our plans called for us to trek on foot the hundred miles from Lake Albert to Juba, the navigable point of the Nile, and then get a boat down the river. But with the Nile in flood, this was impossible. We were also unable to visit Murchison Falls, one of the scenic wonders of that region. We finally reached Juba, where we found Stuffy's boat on which he was to research some of these distant waterways. I turned down his invitation to go along. He intended to spend several weeks on board before returning to Khartoum, where he would report to the British governor.

A lorry took us a few miles north of Juba to Jinga, where we would begin our boat trip. Here, while waiting for our boat to sail, I refused an invitation to stay in the home of the D.C. of Juba. This government representative had already tried to make passes at me when we spent the day in the bush. I was beginning to discover that an unattached female was considered fair game for these lonely men far from their homes.

*Nile boat navigating through sudd, 1929. Mosquito-proof sleeping cages are
perched on upper deck*

⌐

Travel in Africa in the late twenties was slow. With neither air-
planes nor the powerful trucks and jeeps that we have today, it was a
three weeks' trip down the Nile in sternpaddle wheel boats from
Jinga to Khartoum. From there it was to be a train ride around some
of the cataracts of the Nile and by boat again to the Aswan Dam to
pick up another train to Cairo. The main boat we took down the Nile
had to have a low draft and couldn't carry much cargo. At some of
the small landings, we loaded up with logs and brush to feed our
hungry steam engine.

Several barges were attached to the sides of our boats to carry
both the cargo and native passengers traveling from remote areas to
sell their produce or to buy supplies for their families living in the
interior. Whole families were crowded together with their pots and
pans and cook stoves. Bags of rice seemed to be their main diet,
corn, as we moved north. Occasionally, a chicken would have its
neck wrung, but not until it had been fed a few grains of rice.

We drifted along in shallow channels lined with papyrus plants,
which grew in mats floating in the water. The Nile was in flood so
wide that solid land wasn't visible. Our main boat had small, stuffy
cabins on the lower deck. At night we slept in screened cages on the
upper deck, men in one cage and women in the other. Since the only

other women besides me were two nuns returning from their missionary post, I had a cage to myself. The nuns could not appear in such a public setting. I felt sorry for them cooped up below in their long white robes. The only other passengers were Old Misery, a young district commissioner from the Shetland Isles in northern Scotland, and I. We spent our daylight hours in the deck house with the captain, who regaled us with his seafaring tales. The deck was the coolest spot, though our slow speed barely provided a breeze. At night, our navigator somehow followed the channel, guided by instinct, memory, or the stars.

One night at the end of the first week, there was a sudden crunch, followed by the cessation of the splash of the paddle wheels. Silence was succeeded by much yelling from the native crew. We were stuck in the sudd, the great masses of floating papyrus that jammed up the channel, a dreaded hazard in flood time. We were surrounded. Some of the clods seemed as big as small islands. After three days of hard work by the natives unhitching the barges and pushing at the clods, we still couldn't move.

With no radio to call for help, we had to wait for rescue. It was understood that if we didn't reach Khartoum by a certain date, a rescue vessel would be sent out to dynamite the blocking mats of vegetation. At last, on the fourth night, the men freed our boat. With much pushing and shoving, we were finally on our way. Great masses of papyrus pushed ahead of us in a rush. The barges had to be retrieved and attached. A few days later we met the rescue ship that had been sent out to find us. They were much relieved to see that we had freed ourselves.

After the solitude of the Nile, Khartoum was a dizzying experience. Swarms of natives thronged the marketplace. We spent two days in the dirt and dust and heat. The train we boarded for our next leg of the journey was hot and uncomfortable. Having come down with dysentery in Khartoum, I was unable to eat. One of the passengers was a young doctor, who became alarmed at my condition. With no proper medicines with him, he obtained some camel's milk at one of the stops and persuaded me to drink. It was an unforgettable ordeal. Luckily, I recovered enough to board the boat that was to take us on our last leg of the Nile to Aswan. We sailed past Abu Simbel in daylight, not realizing that after the Aswan Dam was built, the lake it formed would flood this whole area and cover the twenty-foot-high statues etched into the sandstone cliffs. Eventually they were removed intact and set on higher ground. How fortunate we were to see them where they had been created.

From Aswan, I continued north by train, stopping to see the tombs of the long-dead Egyptian kings. Still recovering from dysentery, I wasn't fully able to appreciate these wonders. But after resting in a comfortable hotel in Cairo, I was ready to continue my travels.

From this point on, the return trip to London seemed like a travelogue. After Cairo, I went to Jerusalem, where I enjoyed a swim in the Dead Sea. With a car and guide, which the Thomas Cook agents insisted I have for safety, I continued on to Damascus and then to Beirut, where I boarded a freighter. Without the medicines of today, I was still suffering from the food poisoning I had contracted in Khartoum. But I dragged along, vowing not to give in. By the time the freighter called at Constantinople (Istanbul) and Athens, I had recovered enough to enjoy the sights. And when the boat discharged the passengers at Naples, I was finally myself again.

Before completing my sojourn I took a side trip to Sicily to visit the beautiful hilltop resort of Taormina, where my mother had died two years before. Like a pilgrimage, this trip set my heart to rest as I visited the ruins and Mount Etna, which my mother had painted before being stricken with the bronchial pneumonia that took her life. Sadly she had succumbed before she got to Rome, her lifelong ambition.

London and Marriage

L ONDON IN DECEMBER was dreary and cold. Lonely and anxiously awaiting Jock's arrival from Africa, I stayed in a hotel in Piccadilly Circus. Two days later Jock and I were married by a justice of the peace, whose office was on a narrow side street that seemed to have come out of Dickens. The American Vice Consul was a witness to make sure there would be no problem with my American citizenship. His yellow limousine was too big for the street.

After our wedding Jock and I journeyed to Edinburgh to meet his parents. I wasn't sure they liked me. We also visited the graves of his ancestors in northern Scotland. *They* had nothing to say, buried six feet deep, one on top of another. Our honeymoon continued across the ocean, where Jock would have a chance to meet my relatives compliments of Auntie, who had sent us round-trip tickets. What luxury! On our arrival we were greeted like visiting royalty, fêted by friends and family. As they all became acquainted with Jock, they grew to accept him. It was faint approval, but I was relieved. Soon we were happy to return to London to set up our new home in a small boardinghouse. Jock continued to work in his London office, finishing the reports on Northern Rhodesia. We planned to go back to Africa in late summer. We bought a Ford motorcar so we could tour the English countryside when Jock could get away from his work. In the meantime, I explored the museums and historic sites of the city.

Winter in London was gray and foggy. I missed my friends and my work. When an invitation arrived to visit Sunny, an old friend of Mother who was spending the winter near Saint Moritz, I accepted. Switzerland again. Skiing and skating. It was too good to be true. Sunny had rented a house a few miles south of Saint Moritz and moved in with her three small children and their governess. Sunny tutored the children herself; the governess taught them German, and French teachers were hired from the town. The children thrived, learning to skate at a nearby resort and taking ski instruction on the slopes. For entertainment they wrote and performed plays. Little did I know that the youngest boy, Monty, who was eight at the time, was laying the groundwork for a future acting career. I can remember him, standing at the height of land, gazing toward Italy, his right arm across his chest, as he soliloquized, "I am Napoleon going to conquer the world." Later, as Montgomery Clift, Monty became a movie star and won the hearts of millions.

From left, Kay in Saint Moritz with Clift children, Montgomery, Brooks, and Sister (Ethel), 1930

In Saint Moritz I was in my element. I enjoyed skating, skiing, and tobogganing as much as the kids. Apparently, my enthusiasm left an impression. In a biography of Montgomery Clift by Patricia Bosworth, which I read years later, his older brother Brooks was quoted as saying, "Kate Billings was our only friend. Kate was a jolly, young, twenty-three-year-old American geologist, fresh from two years in Africa."

The following summer, the first of my marriage, Baldie, the Bryn Mawr classmate who had driven with me to Wyoming in the old Model A Ford, was doing some research at a London hospital. She persuaded me to drive her and a friend on a trip through northern Europe. Since I had planned to take a geological excursion in the Chamonix region, she and her friend agreed to bring the car across the English Channel by ferry. Although we met in Rotterdam, Holland, she waited until we had reached Belgium before breaking the news that Jock had entrusted to her. He had been assigned to the Gold Coast (Ghana) in West Africa by the British Geological Survey. The British forbade the geologists from taking wives to this part of the world and he had signed a contract agreeing to their terms. I was in an awful dilemma, feeling very anxious about my future. I left the two women with the car and returned to London to talk things over with Jock.

The Woman Who Dressed Like a Man

THE NEWS had shattered all my dreams of being a partner and helper in Jock's geological work. Now my future was at stake. I was certainly not going to sit around London waiting for Jock's tour to be over. I would plan my own career and find some place in West Africa where I could do my own geological research. The land was vast. I settled on Sierra Leone as my destination. It was a small country, just north of the equator, no bigger than New England. Sierra Leone was long considered a land with no mineral resources. Then, in 1928, two years before, everything changed. Gold and iron had been discovered, a chromium mine was under investigation, diamonds had just been found, and platinum was being extricated from gravels along the coast. To be sure, it was still known as the "white man's grave." Many of the colonial officers who were sent out to manage the government, as well as many other white people, had died there. Sierra Leone was an English protectorate, the oldest of the British Crown colonies. The British had purchased the vicinity of the port of Freetown, the capital, from the native king in the late 1700s and used it as a place to send freed slaves. The interior was declared a protectorate and was a buffer zone to prevent French encroachment from Guinea in the north.

I read all the literature about Sierra Leone and talked to some people who had been there. There were a few roads, a thousand miles in all, and a railroad to reach from Freetown into the interior. The British had surveyed the country and produced a set of topographic maps. I decided I would travel by train and car to all the accessible areas to look over the land before choosing a place for geological field study. Jock was in full agreement. I would take the Ford on my journey and we could board the same boat for West Africa.

As I began to plan my trip, a British mines department was being set up in Freetown to take care of the growing interest in mining. We met the young man who was leaving shortly to head this bureau. He assured me there would be no problem in my exploring at will. He said they would welcome a knowledgeable scientist, even a woman, and he would do what he could to help me. I found that the London School of Hygiene offered a course in tropical medicine, so I enrolled in order to learn about diseases and the necessary precautions for life in the tropics. In class I was educated about taking five grains of quinine every evening to prevent malaria and covering myself with netting in the evenings to avoid mosquito bites. I learned about what clothes to wear and the necessity of boiling water. Dr. Stammers, our instructor, was most helpful when I told him I would be going off trails into the bush. He taught us that all snakes were to be considered poisonous and advised that I take snake serum. Since I had allergies, he sent me to a doctor to determine if I was horse-sensitive. I was found to be allergic and given instructions on how to inject the serum slowly, over intervals, drop by drop, followed by the administration of adrenaline.

In preparation for my trip, I painted the inside of my army helmet with aluminum to reflect some of the sun's rays and to keep my head cool. Tropical outfitters made "spine pads" for my lightweight, khaki wool shirt. These were padded triangles that buttoned on the back of my shirt to provide extra protection from the sun's rays from neck to lower spine. I had shorts made with six-inch cuffs that could be buttoned up high on my legs or lowered to protect them, and custom-made lightweight, but sturdy, hobnailed boots. I even had time to have a mechanic teach me the basics of auto repair since there were no garages *en route*. I certainly hoped I would not have to rely upon my rudimentary skills.

In Liverpool the outfitters prepared a dozen wooden crates, each packed with a variety of foods, from powdered milk to tins of meat and crackers, salt and sugar. Each would be a two weeks' supply of essentials. Everything I would use had to be brought out from England. Two tin trunks were obtained for my clothing. I also ordered a small tent, a cot, a chair, a table, a canvas tub and basin, all made of mold-resistant canvas, with collapsible wooden parts to fit into small bundles. With this flotilla of supplies, I was well prepared for trekking anywhere into the bush and camping. It would be a far different life from that I had experienced doing my thesis work in the Laramie Mountains. In Sierra Leone I would have to be self-sufficient for weeks at a time, with a retinue of natives to care for me.

At last Jock and I were both ready to sail from Liverpool. The Ford was swung into the hold of the ship, our goods were put on board, and we were off for the eleven-day voyage to Freetown. It was time to relax and adjust to the increasing heat and humidity as we steamed toward the equator.

Freetown at last! The anchor was dropped in the bay as thunder roared across "the mountains of the lion." Sierra Leone was aptly

"The Gold Missus," Sierra Leone, 1930

named. The heavy downpour was not an auspicious beginning. When the rains stopped, the heat and humidity pressed in on us. Barges appeared and were quickly loaded by cranes that swung out from our boat with the goods stored in the hold. I watched anxiously until at last I saw the Ford emerge, deposited on a heaving flat-topped boat just large enough to hold it. Securely fastened by ropes, the car was taken off to the wharf.

Fode (left) and Amadu with Buster, Sierra Leone, 1930

A customs officer appeared and checked the passports of those who were debarking. A small launch came alongside and to my relief, the head of the British Mines Department came aboard. I was to go ashore with him and he would see to my goods. He had brought an invitation from a woman in the Education Department who was out from England to supervise the schools in the region. I was delighted to stay with her and get organized for my trip into the interior.

Once ashore, I was ushered to a waiting car past all the hubbub of swarming natives and the mounds of goods still coming from our boat. My friend said one of his clerks would take charge of clearing my Ford and personal boxes through customs. We drove through the crowded town, past the huge cottonwood tree, which was the central gathering place. I was already limp from the heat. The smells were nauseating. I felt better as we rose out of the town to more open space, where I could breathe. After passing the shanties characteristic of the lower village, small wooden houses appeared in clusters. Higher on the slopes, cement dwellings had been built, raised above the ground to eliminate the damp and mildew that came from the mists of the tropics. These houses belonged to the white people who did business in the colony.

My host turned into a driveway lined with palm trees and bananas and stopped at the entrance, whose door was half hidden behind a purple bougainvillea. Out stepped my hostess, Miss Carey, cool and comfortable in her white dress. She greeted us cordially and served chilled drinks as she told of her work in organizing the district schools. I was left in her charge while my friend went off to attend to my goods.

The next ten days were delightful. The British colony of whites who lived on the hillside were friendly and anxious to hear about the latest news from England. The women ran their households with servants to do the shopping and cleaning while their husbands had jobs in town. Most of their older children were away at boarding schools or with relatives in England. It was considered too unhealthy a climate to raise the young. The wives stayed for a few months, returning home when the heat and humidity took a toll on their health. For entertainment they had clubs or gave dinner parties for their husbands.

The women couldn't understand how I would dare to go into the bush or stay out in the tropical heat. How could I live amongst strange natives with the risks of the jungle? There were leopards and snakes to contend with. I assured them I knew what I was facing. I had traveled the African continent from tip to toe and had visited the camps of other geologists, men to be sure. I had also worked alone in Wyoming with no natives to care for me. That seemed more arduous than what I now faced.

Despite the comforts, I was anxious to leave this life of leisure and start work on my own. But it took days to clear my goods from customs through governmental red tape. Nobody hurries in West Africa. Time seems to stand still.

There remained a number of important tasks to be accomplished. First, I had to have servants. I could not go without a personal "boy" and a cook. Miss Carey was very helpful. Word went out through her servants that "Missus" wanted reliable helpers. The next morning a crowd of hopefuls appeared, some with letters of recommendation from former employers. Miss Carey spotted one frail-looking boy whom she knew and advised me to hire him. His name was Amadu. He had previously worked for a missus and was disliked by the others for his loyalty to his employer. When his missus was sick in the hospital, he had commandeered all the hot water for her bath and secured luxuries from the kitchen. He had proved that he would be faithful. Choosing a cook was more difficult. The best ones were obviously already employed. We picked out Fode. He had a sneaky look about him but he would have to do.

Ten days later I was ready to board the train. The Ford had been loaded on a flatcar two days earlier and sent ahead to Kenema, where I would start my tour of the country. The keys had been sealed in an envelope and I had seen them deposited on a shelf in front of the engineer, the safest place I was told. They had to accompany the car.

I was at the station at six in the morning hunting for Amadu and Fode in the mass of milling natives. Already it was hot and humid. I found them beside two huge wooden crates. Their goods, they said. They had been told they could each bring a small bundle. Since there would be no room in the Ford, these boxes had to be left in Freetown; whatever could be put in a bundle went with us.

On the train a first-class compartment had been provided for me and my possessions. This proved to be an empty baggage car, since white men traveled with chairs and tables. Amadu and Fode extracted my chair from my luggage and expertly put it together. My small table was also found. So, with picnic box beside me, I sat and waited. Curious faces stared through the open sides of the car. Amadu and Fode took off to the crowded third-class section to spend the day chatting with their friends. At every stop they checked to see what I needed.

At last we were off. The clerk from the Mines Department saluted smartly, glad to see the last of me. It had been his responsibility to take care of all the details of my journey. The train jerked and jolted as we rounded the edge of the peninsula, then crossed the mangrove swamps on the north on a scary-looking trestle to reach the protectorate. There was no road out of Freetown. Traveling eastward we passed through the jungle, with glimpses of high trees decorated with rope-like creepers that hung to the ground, an impenetrable mass of solid green leaves below. Then we came to open spaces of low bush that had been carved out of the forest, cutover areas used for farming and then abandoned after only a few years. Again we came to the thick forest, a tangle of bushes and small struggling trees. Once it was cut over it would never be virgin mahogany forest again.

Whistling and puffing, the engine stopped at small villages, where noisy crowds of natives greeted us. Curious faces stared as I sat, hot and tired, in my empty freight car. I had wondered how the trip of 136 miles could take all day! I was learning. At one point the train stopped with a jerk. Pandemonium. The natives poured from their cars and rushed into the bush. I was sure there had been an accident.

Sierra Leone, 1930

But they soon returned carrying a buck that had been hit by the train and wounded. It had fled, only to be captured by the excited crowd.

It was dark when we finally arrived at Bo, our destination for the night. A thunderstorm was in progress. There was a rest house near the station. Dripping and wet I ran to the shelter, leaving Amadu and Fode to collect my goods. They had found plenty of natives anxious to earn a few pennies to bring in my loads. Amadu took charge. He had them set up my chair and bed in the center of the room. Like all the rest houses I would encounter, it was unfurnished. There was one large main room, with kitchen shelter outside. A cubicle, which served as a bathroom, had no running water. After I had "bathed" or sponged, I put on pajamas and boots made of soft suede to protect me from the malarial mosquitoes. Then I took five grains of quinine and ate a meal that had been quickly assembled from canned goods out of my boxes. I crawled under my mosquito net and into bed.

It was still dark when Amadu came in with a lantern to wake me. I dressed quickly, ate a hurried breakfast of orange juice, tea, and toast prepared by Fode, and was off on the early train for the forty-four miles to Kenema. Here, I was met by Mr. Brown, the assistant D.C. of the region. He had a dozen prisoners with him who took charge of my loads. They piled them in the middle of a large, white cement rest house, which was thatched with a conically shaped roof. A black mamba, a deadly poisonous snake, was found coiled in a corner. With much shouting and running the beast was driven outside. The watchman finally beheaded it with a sharp-edged machete, a versatile tool used by all the natives for many different jobs.

Brown, as he preferred to be called, took me back to the railroad where my Ford was reposing on a flatcar on a siding. Then he asked for the keys. We soon discovered they had disappeared in transit and Jock had gone off with the extra set on his key ring. It would take weeks to contact him in the bush on the Gold Coast where he was working. Some method of getting into the car had to be devised. After three days of tinkering, Brown had the prisoners bodily remove the automobile from the flatcar. It was costing fifteen dollars a day for it to sit there. Finally, Brown located a clever native who had tools with which he opened the car. No doubt his trade was thievery, for he turned out to be very adept. But he knew nothing about engines. A Syrian lorry driver tackled the job. He fussed with wires and connections and finally announced the car would start by simply connecting two wires. Lo and behold, it did.

In the meantime, I was entertained by Brown and the head district commissioner. In the daytime I walked the trails in the area studying the rocks of the region. A "court messenger" was assigned to act as my guard and guide. Sometimes Brown and I played tennis in the late afternoon. At other times we had target practice. Brown wanted the natives to know that Missus had a gun and was a good shot. Word would get around. The head D.C. was about to leave for a three months' vacation in England. He placed his dog Buster, a mixed Airedale breed, into my charge. She looked big and ferocious and would keep strangers at bay.

At length I was ready to leave. The car was loaded for an early morning start. At dawn, Amadu appeared in great excitement. The ants were eating my car! "Wreaths" of black ants covered the tires, supposedly consuming the rubber. A crowd had collected to watch. As the sun rose, the crowd roared. We watched in fascination as lines of black ants marched away. They had simply swarmed over the tires for warmth and spent a cozy night.

The D.C. insisted that I take a court messenger to guard me. I told him the man would have to be thin in order to squeeze into the back of the car with all the luggage and Buster. Amadu and Fode would sit in front. The bulk of my goods, including my tent, were left in Kenema. Along the route I would stay in the rest houses built for travelers. I had also learned about local foods. So long as I kept near the roads in this part of the country, I could live off the land with very few extras to be supplied from my one "chop box." Abou, the court messenger who accompanied me, was small and slim. He knew the local language of this part of the protectorate and proved invaluable in bargaining for food with the native chiefs. There were more than thirteen different tribes in Sierra Leone. Each had its own language, so it was important to have an interpreter along.

First, we headed for a chain of nearby hills, where a chromium deposit had been found. Prospectors were already at work, hoping that it would become profitable. There was a small town at the foot of the mountains where I found a shop owned by a Frenchman who belonged to a syndicate of shopkeepers with stores scattered along the main roads to trade with the natives.

I was able to leave the Ford in the company shed while I trekked to the mine. Notified of my visit, the miner had sent carriers to meet me. They took charge of my personal goods. I had to bring everything, including my bed. At last we set off, single file, on a narrow trail. In time we reached a small village hidden away in the bush. As

Chief with retinue, Sierra Leone, 1931

we approached, a crowd appeared, noisy and shouting. Abou took charge. The chief of the village, a woman, had come out to greet me. We touched hands and grinned at each other while Abou translated. She presented me with a "calabash" of food: rice, vegetables, oranges, and a live rooster. A gift was customary. In return, I "dashed" her three shillings. Abou returned one of the coins to me, saying it was too much. With my servants already heavily loaded, the native carrying my gift was sent with me to the mine.

This was my introduction to the routine that ensued at every village when a white man was on trek. Abou explained that there were not many women chiefs. Inheritance was through the eldest sister of a chief. If she had no children, she became chief. The smaller villages had a headman, who was responsible to the chief of the largest village in the area, who in turn, was under the paramount chief. The paramount chief collected the five-shilling head tax for the government, which was then given to the D.C. of the area.

The paramount chief was the most powerful in the hierarchy of chiefs and headmen in the country. He controlled the farms and was in charge of selling the produce, mostly rice and peanuts, in Freetown. The price was higher than "up country." Wherever I went, much time was spent meeting these leaders, always with much palaver. A white woman traveling alone was a curiosity. Years later I learned that these natives had dubbed me "the woman who dressed like a man." Many had never seen a white woman in the hinterland where I traveled. Everywhere the villagers turned out to gape.

We parted at last from the woman chief and continued our route to the mine. A steep trail ascended through the forest to a small cleared area. Here, four small huts had been constructed for the use of Smith, the miner in charge. I was assigned the room in the half of the largest building, where my goods were deposited.

The next day Smith showed me around the ditches and trenches that crisscrossed the ore. A few loads had already been sent out to Freetown to be tested, to see if the mine would be profitable. I spent three days in the area, studying the deposits, going back and forth across the hilly region.

The soil in these moist tropics was deep. The rocks had been leached by the process of "weathering" until a red crust was formed that contained ferruginous minerals with various amounts of aluminum and a few insoluble remnants of the original rock. Called laterite, the crust completely disguised the rocks from which it was derived. It was obvious I had to follow the streams and gullies to make any conclusions about the geology. Staying close to the roads and trails would teach me little. Perhaps I would return at a later date to these hills and explore them in greater detail.

But first I had to journey further and get a broader view of the protectorate. Then I had to settle down to work on a particular project. Leaving the mine, we returned to the road to pick up my car. I spent several more weeks exploring before reaching Sefadu at the northern end of the road. Miss Carey planned to meet me there.

One of my stops along the route was at Kailahun, on the Meli River, where the boundaries of French Guinea and Liberia met with Sierra Leone. This was one of the few remaining places in Africa where barter was done with tokens, "Kissi pennies," thin iron rods sixteen inches long, twisted and forged by hand. They were used in all three countries as the currency of the region. A dozen were equal to a shilling. It was a common sight to see a native coming to market carrying on his head a squealing pig tied up in raffia. Later, he would be seen returning with a bundle of Kissi pennies. As mining came into the country, this barter system changed overnight. I was fortunate to be there before the native customs gave way to development.

Finally, it was almost Christmas, and I drove north to Sefadu in high, open country. We left behind the forested areas for a region covered with elephant grass thirteen feet high. Picturesque, bare, rounded hills called inselbergs appeared.

At Sefadu the D.C.'s house stood on a knoll surrounded by landscaped gardens. A high, thatched roof capped the whitewashed walls

Rest house at Sefadu with "elephant" boulder, Sierra Leone, Christmas, 1930

of his dwelling. Miss Carey was to meet me here in a few days. Lane, the D.C. of the area, told me he had invited the six white men who worked in the vicinity, mostly traders, to join us over Christmas. They would be housed in grass shimbeks with sides made of palm leaves from the garden. The shimbeks were hastily constructed beyond the rest house, which Miss Carey and I would occupy.

On Christmas Eve Miss Carey arrived. The cooks prepared a sumptuous Christmas feast, a little bit of England with a decidedly tropical touch. She had brought a huge box filled with perishable goods preserved in ice and packed in sawdust. Included were a turkey, some fish, fresh tomatoes, and even cranberries. All had come by boat from England.

Miss Carey also brought a letter for me from the Mines Department head asking if I would make a study and a map of the iron ore that had been discovered in a range of hills in the center of the protectorate. I was to go to Magburaka, near the end of the northern prong of the railroad. He would send me a headman, Johnny Boy, who had trekked with white men before. Johnny Boy would take charge of my carriers, who could be found in the vicinity.

I jumped at the chance to tackle this assignment. By this time I was acclimated to the tropics and had learned how to tolerate the heat and humidity. I had become accustomed to the laterite and tropical soils and I had lived off the land. I understood the native customs of meeting the chiefs of the villages, having palaver, and exchanging gifts or dash. In my favor was having studied the iron ores on the Lake Superior trip in Wisconsin. That excursion had given me the confidence that I needed to tackle this job.

After we left Sefadu, Miss Carey drove with me as far as Bo, where she boarded the train to Freetown. We had driven the hundred and fifty miles from Sefadu in nine and a half hours. The loads and tent that I had left in Kenema were forwarded by train to meet me. Fode was to accompany them as there was no room for him in the crowded car. I said good-bye to Miss Carey. Abou, my court messenger, was to return to his headquarters in Kenema.

<

Amadu, Buster, and I set out from Bo in my Ford in the early morning to travel the ninety miles north to Magburaka. Along the route we had to ford rivers. By late afternoon I reached the rest house, where I awaited my loads from Kenema as well as further instructions from the Mines Department.

The government had closed a large area north of Magburaka to prospecting, including the range of hills where iron ore had been discovered two years before by a government geologist. I would spend several weeks mapping the deposit, collecting samples, and exploring the range. A court messenger named Momo Limba would accompany me. He could speak the dialect of the region and could deal with the native chiefs and see that they supplied me with food.

After two days' waiting in the hottest place I had yet been, the train arrived with Fode and my loads from Kenema. Johnny Boy appeared smiling. He promptly took charge of sorting my goods so they could be taken in the Ford to Mabonto, ten miles away. It took two trips to transport my retinue and some of the goods. The bulky boxes went by lorry.

At Mabonto, the chief was most helpful. A "bari" or central meeting place had just been built in the middle of the village. The chief thought it would be just the place for me to leave the Ford when I went on trek. Such a fine car should not be left in the open. He had one of the sides of the bari removed and I drove the Ford in. The wall was promptly replaced. The car could be admired by all through the open sides of the bari. The chief grinned broadly when I said I would give him a ride on my return.

A whole day was spent in sorting my goods into seventy-pound loads. Johnny Boy decided I would need sixteen carriers. Word went out that Missus was going on trek and needed help. Dozens of natives appeared that afternoon hoping for a job. With Momo Limba and Johnny Boy's help, we looked them over, eliminating all but twenty. These I carefully screened, choosing ones who had sturdy necks to support a load and no sores on their hands or legs. The chosen sixteen were told to come at dawn bringing only a small bundle of their necessary belongings.

The next morning, bright and early, the goods were all lined up: tent, bed and bed roll, boxes of food, kerosene in a five-gallon tin for my lanterns, and two tin trunks all ready to load. The carriers appeared and chose their loads with no squabbling. Johnny Boy helped place the loads on their heads, which were protected by rolls of cloth or grass. Off they went, single file, with villagers watching. Johnny Boy strode behind, feeling very important. Momo Limba and I came last, with a small boy whom Momo Limba had corralled to carry my knapsack, hammer, and notebook. I was not allowed to carry anything, he informed me. He would accompany me and carry me across any streams, as the snails in the waters carried diseases. I also had to keep my boots dry or they would disintegrate rapidly with mold in the tropics. My carriers wore sneakers or sandals made from old tires. Many were barefoot.

It was fifteen miles north to the village of Nerekoro. Johnny Boy went ahead to set up my camp. I lingered behind to study the rocks. Late in the day I arrived, hot and tired. I found my small tent set up at the edge of the village under a large tulip tree, whose red blossoms were strewn on the ground. Two dilapidated huts were close by. Out from the fly of my tent wandered a goat and several chickens. I was furious. This was not far enough away from the village. It would be noisy and it was unhealthy to be around those animal droppings. Mosquitoes were infected by biting a malaria-carrying native. The insects in turn could pass it on to me. It was too late to move camp that day. I berated Johnny Boy. Never again did he make camp so close to a village. An area outside any camp had to be "brushed" with machetes, leaving a large open space on ground completely cleared. The carriers could walk to the villages; I would stay alone with a watchman.

Getting to sleep proved difficult. Scavengers came in from the forest to gather what scraps they could find. I had been told that wild cats and leopards were in the area. The watchman stationed outside my tent kept a small fire burning to keep marauders away. Finally, I dozed off only to be awakened by the loud beat of tom-toms. They

Tent in the bush, Sierra Leone, ca. 1931

kept echoing through my brain. Momo Limba, who had decided to sleep outside my tent, arose and went into the village. The drums stopped, and I finally slept.

The next day, I sent the men ahead to a village twelve miles distant with instructions to Johnny Boy to make camp "far from village." Momo Limba and I dropped down to the river below to seek out a gold prospector who was said to be in the vicinity. We found him, a grizzled old man panning gold in the river. He had very little cash for this adventure, but was optimistic that he would make a fortune. He had no idea how to live in the tropics. I later learned that he became ill with malaria a few days after we saw him and had to be carried out and sent back to Freetown. From there, penniless and ill, he was sent back to England as a DBS, Deported British Subject.

It was because of such men that the British Mines Department decided to close a large area where gold had been reported. They feared a gold rush with indigent people stampeding out to search for their fortunes. A company from England called the Maroc, Ltd., was granted a concession to explore that area and develop any prospects they found. Thus the government could have mining developed under supervision. The venture would also be more profitable for Sierra Leone.

Likewise, in the eastern part of the country, where diamonds had been found, a large area was closed to independent prospectors and a concession granted to an American firm. The government wanted to prevent fortune hunters from invading the country. For this reason, they awaited my report on the iron ore possibilities before deciding what to do about the closed area I was exploring. I was lucky to be a partner in this policy.

I progressed northward slowly, moving camp about twelve miles a day and keeping track of the geology on the way. Fode provided me with tasty food. Stews were made largely of groundnuts or "peanuts" and chicken. Bananas and oranges were plentiful until we reached drier regions, where the fruit trees were unable to grow. Hot tea three times a day was preferable to lukewarm drinks. Water always had to be boiled a minimum of five minutes. Thermoses were filled every day with boiled water for tea for my trail lunches. Rice was the food of the country, raised in cutover areas on the hillside. In the north it became scarcer, as the new crop had not been picked.

Momo Limba was helpful in convincing the natives to sell me enough rice to feed the carriers. With persuasion, he could buy me a skinny chicken, or even an egg. At breakfast one day there was no salt. I had purchased a pound in Magburaka and could not possibly have consumed it all. Fode's integrity had always seemed dubious. This was the final straw. He was dismissed from the camp immediately; a disgruntled cook was known to poison his master's food. Amadu told me later that Fode had sold the salt to the carriers over a period of time, thinking I would never notice.

A runner was sent off to Magburaka to ask the district commissioner to find me another cook. Ten days later a tall, smiling man with excellent credentials arrived to relieve Amadu from his feeble attempts to feed me.

"Harmattan" winds from the desert were drying up the grass of this northern region and grass fires became common. The natives were in the habit of setting fires to make open space for their spring planting. We had crossed areas that had been burned over and found green grass appearing only a week or so after the fires had passed. It was becoming stifling in the heat. Haze and smoke filled the air.

Villages were spaced miles apart in the dry country. One night we had to camp five miles from a small village. We set up camp along a small stream in the tall grass. The men refused to sleep in the open and it was too far to walk five miles to the village. Instead they trampled down a small area near my clearing and quickly built a shimbek of grass and palm leaves as a makeshift shelter.

In the middle of the night I awoke to the sound of crackling and the smell of smoke in the stifling heat. Instantly I realized the danger. The carriers were already alerted. They rushed from their shimbek and began trampling and cutting down the grass in our vicinity. They piled heaps of it in the open space down wind from the hiss and sputter, setting fire to the cuttings and making backfires to the stream. Our empty five-gallon tins were filled with water. Amadu and Momo Limba kept pouring water on my tent so that sparks would not ignite it. The flames jumped across the stream and made their way around our clearing. Finally, the danger was past. That night I dreamed that I was back in Montana. A fire flashback!

As I worked northward, the laterite on the hills became more ferruginous. Near villages I found small diggings with the remains of piles of the laterite near what appeared to be abandoned kilns. Here the chiefs had smelted the rock to make iron weapons, a custom since forbidden by the British. The chiefs were loath to lead me to those places for fear they would be reported.

One day I came to a high hill covered with a crust of dark-red laterite. This had to be the place where iron ore had been reported. The whole slope was of high-grade quality, far better than the laterite that the natives had used. I spent some time taking samples and wondered about the rocks from which they had been derived. In a small gully I found the answer. High-quality iron ore was sandwiched between sandstone layers. With digging and searching, I found it to be almost a foot in width. This was the clue I had been seeking. The iron ore had weathered into this wide capping of workable ore.

I decided to try to follow these beds of sandstone interbedded with several layers of high-grade ore. The rocks appeared to be standing on end. Uplift of the original sediments followed by years of erosion had put them in this position. They were now concealed by laterite soil. They seemed to point south to form the backbone of the hills that rose above the river.

For the next few weeks I worked southward, making camp in the valley. I did daily traverses across the ridge of hills. Half a dozen of my carriers went ahead of me and slashed down the creepers with their machetes so I could pass. I was able to find fresh outcroppings in small rivulets and gullies high up on the ridge. The layers of rocks continued to have beds of sandstone and iron ore. In places the layers were wide enough to mine. Because of the distance from the coast, these deposits might prove unprofitable, but at least I had the answer to the origin of the highly ferruginous laterite of these hills. I had been able to trace these beds for thirty-six miles.

One day, as I neared Nerekoro, a messenger appeared with a telegram from the Mines Department. It said tersely: "Urgent. Return Freetown immediately." There was no further explanation. I had to go. Since I couldn't get a train from Magburaka for at least three days, I decided to visit Maranda, where a gold mine had just opened. I could make a small detour on my way to Mabonto to pick up my car.

The next afternoon we reached Maranda, where a row of small huts stood on a hill overlooking the placer mine. I had the men set up my tent not far from the village, which was a short walk from the mine. When the four white men returned from supervising the placer workings and heard about my arrival, they promptly sent me an invitation to dine with them that night. Tired as I was, I could not refuse. They were cordiality itself. I took my leave early and was soon asleep under my mosquito net in the middle of the bush that I had come to love. My watchman was crouched outside by his fire.

Some time later I awoke with a start, my head exploding with the dreaded sound of the tom-toms. A dance was in progress only a short distance away. After fifteen minutes I felt my skull would split open. I was desperate. This noise had to be stopped. I crawled out from under the net and slipped on my mosquito boots. I put a raincoat on over my pajamas, grabbed a flashlight, and awoke the watchman. He refused to stir from his fire. Then I stomped down the trail to the village with Buster close at my heels.

In the large village square, surrounded by a ring of pointed thatched huts, a mob of native men was dancing to the rhythm of the loud, beating drums. The moonlight cast an eerie glow on the scene. I hesitated a moment, but was determined to stop the unnerving noise of the tom-toms. I blew three blasts on my whistle. The tom-toms stopped. Confronted by a crowd of fierce faces, I saw hatred in their eyes as they faced me in dead silence. There was no Momo Limba or Amadu to support me and there were no women in the crowd. For a moment I was paralyzed with fear, but I had to go through with this.

In a loud voice I cried out, "You must stop this noise. You should know better than to have a dance when a white woman is camped by your village. Go to another village, anywhere, but stop these tom-

toms." Dead silence followed. The faces came nearer. I stood my ground, waiting. Finally, a man clad in white stepped out from the crowd, doffed his round, white cap, bowed twice, and said, "Yes, Missus. We 'gree for stop." He turned to the crowd and spoke a few words to the tense group as I stood waiting silently. Slowly the crowd turned away, muttering as they dispersed. Finally, I walked back to my tent, dazed and shaking, realizing what a fool I had been to face this mob alone.

The next morning we arose before dawn. There was no sign of life as we filed through the village. The mining camp was still asleep. I sent the carriers by a shorter route to Mabonto. They would meet me that afternoon. Taking Johnny Boy and the trusty boy who carried my hammer and knapsack, I crossed the high hills to the east of Maranda. Two carriers with machetes cleared the bush in my path.

In Mabonto I paid off the carriers, had the tires of the Ford blown up, and removed the car from the bari. Since the chief was away, I couldn't give him the ride I had promised. I hired a lorry to take what wouldn't fit into the Ford and drove to Magburaka. Many tall natives, dressed in flowing white gowns with turbans on their heads, watched me silently. There seemed to be a feeling of unrest among the natives, who were looking askance at these northern intruders.

I drove on to Magburaka and went to the D.C.'s office to see if he could explain why I had been ordered to return. I found that all white persons had gone back to Freetown. I sent a telegram to the Mines Department to see whether I should bring the Ford back with me. The reply came back: "Leave loads and car Magburaka."

Momo Limba had to remain at his station in Magburaka. Before we parted, he told me that the tom-tom dance at Maranda was for the feast of the eve of Ramadan. The natives were in a highly emotional state. They had received permission from the four miners to celebrate. My interference was unheard of and I was lucky not to have been cut down by the angry mob. My "juju" must be very powerful, he said. If I had known more about their religion, I never would have interrupted the dance.

I took Amadu, Buster, and the cook with me when I went back to Freetown. The hot train trip seemed unbearable. Throngs of natives peered in at me, sitting alone with Buster, in my empty freight car. They were sullen and unfriendly, not the cheerful smiling faces I had seen on my trip north so many months before.

In Freetown I was met by the head of the Mines Department, relieved to see me safe. He related that there had been an uprising in the north. Adara, a Muslim from French Guinea, had incited the natives. He came with an army and promised the natives he would free them from British rule and the white man's oppression. He proclaimed himself another Mohammed and said that he was immortal. As he marched south, he collected many followers. Troops from Freetown were rushed to meet these hordes. A battleship had just arrived in the harbor to protect the vulnerable colony, for there were many Muslims in Freetown. If Adara was successful, they might rise against the white people.

At last news came that Adara was dead, killed in a skirmish with the British troops led by young Lieutenant Holmes at a stream crossing. Holmes had gone ahead with a small contingent and was himself ambushed and killed. His white sergeant had emptied his revolver in the midst of the attackers as the British retreated across the stream. One lucky shot killed Adara. Without a leader, the revolt fizzled out.

In Freetown I again stayed with Miss Carey. It was strange to be back in civilization. My bush life seemed like a dream. Two weeks later it was safe to return to pick up my car and some personal goods at Magburaka.

For my next foray I had decided to head north to Kaballa, the northernmost outpost of the protectorate. Located high in the hills, it had a healthy climate, where I could rest. I could write the report on my mapping of the iron ores and the tracing of the ore-bearing rocks. The specimens I had collected would be studied in the Mines Department to supplement my findings.

I took the train back to Magburaka to pick up my car and goods. Amadu, Buster, and the cook went with me. First, I made a long day's side trip due west on a very poor road to visit an iron mine that had recently been opened at Marampa. It was a two days' trek from Port Lokko, a town on an estuary of the coast. I left the car. The mine was being run by two white men who had trenched across a round hill covered with very rich ore. Because of its closeness to the small harbor of Port Lokko, ore could easily be shipped out to England. It was not as far off in the interior as the iron beds I had followed. The ore itself had a different origin. It could be worked as a single body because it encompassed the entire hill. It even continued far into the depths of the earth.

Returning east to the rail head where I had left my car, I spent the night at the rest house and then drove north to Kaballa. The Ford was loaded with my personal belongings, Buster and the cook in back, and Amadu beside me. It took eight hours on narrow and hazardous roads, with several rickety bridges to cross, before we reached Kaballa. Here we saw the picturesque pointed thatched roof of the rest house perched high on the top of a hill. We had driven from the green jungle and forests into wide open country, passing through orchard bush and elephant grass. We were surrounded by high, rounded granite peaks that extended far off into the distance. Most of these peaks rose to a height of about 3,000 feet. The highest in the northern province, Bintimani, was said to be more than 6,000 feet high. I wished I had time to climb it.

A well-laid-out barracks was situated in an open space below the large, white rest house where I was staying. The rest house was round, with verandas on every side. I could follow the shade during my stay, enjoying a different view of the round hills from morning to evening as I moved the table around the veranda to escape the hot sun.

The day after my arrival, the locusts descended on the region, darkening the sky as they approached with a strange roaring sound. They consumed everything in sight, leaving the trees leafless, with only green fruit still hanging from branches. The lush green of the carefully tended grass around the buildings and the lovely flower gardens were now a thing of the past.

The end of the dry season was approaching. The rains would descend in earnest, making roads impassable and life in the forests intolerable. April was upon us. After ten days of writing and resting, I was ready to return to Freetown. First, I would stop south of Magburaka and trek to the gold mine at Makong, which was located in the middle of the area that had been given as a concession to the English company to open up placer mines.

Parking the car at Matotaka, I trekked the twenty miles to reach the new mine at Makong. This was the longest hike I had attempted. It was hot and humid. There were several rivers to cross by ferry or fording. One of the native carriers I had taken with me rode me piggyback across streams. The mine itself consisted of several small mud huts, hastily constructed for the comfort of the three white men who were developing the placer mine. They assigned me one of the huts and insisted I eat with them. The man in charge was Mr. Babcock, whom I had previously met in London. He showed me around the trenches where they were sluicing the gold. Already it was proving to be a rich region.

Returning to Matotaka, I drove south to Bo. Here I returned Buster to a court messenger, who would take her to the D.C.'s. house to await her master, who was returning shortly from England. At Bo, the Ford was loaded on a flatcar and sent on to Freetown.

I was to make one more excursion to see the platinum workings on the coast, in the Freetown Colony. The train ride back to Freetown was hot and humid. The rains were just beginning and the forests looked damp and uninviting. A musky odor pervaded everything. I got off the train at a small station on the northern side of the peninsula of Freetown. Amadu, the cook, and I were met by a native policeman, who had been sent to trek with me as a safety precaution. There were six carriers to transport loads to the platinum workings. We climbed to the top of the mountains of the lion, the backbone of the range. After two thousand feet of rough hiking, we reached the top of the pass just as the daily thunderstorm burst upon us. The mountains really roared. By the time we reached the rest house, we were enveloped in mist and rain.

The next morning bright sunshine cleared away the clouds. We descended through the steamy forest to the coast, where we found the platinum diggings. Great boulders were being lifted from a small stream bed. The gravels beneath were carefully sifted to find the rare platinum nuggets that lay at the bottom of the gravel on top of the underlying rock. The torrential rains of the region were wearing down the mountains as the streams rushed down to the sea, carrying the precious platinum along with the boulders and gravel. A study of the high mountain chain would be interesting; perhaps I should consider this as a future project. The source of the platinum was hidden in the hills.

After leaving the platinum diggings, it took us two days to reach Freetown. We trekked across hot sandy beaches and past picturesque fishing villages. The natives here were sophisticated Creoles descended from slaves. They were surly and sullen. I was glad to have the policeman to protect me. He carried a gun and his belt was lined with bullets. How different from my court messenger in the interior, who carried a small baton as his sign of authority.

Outside Freetown I was met by a lorry that had been sent to take me and my loads into town. In Freetown I found that the Mines Department head was in the hospital and Miss Carey was away on government business. I was told the rest house was full. There was nothing to do but stay in the one hotel in town. My room was stifling hot and musty; the noise from the bar below was unbearable. The floor of my room was dirty and the mosquito net over the large double bed was torn. There was no modern plumbing. I had Amadu set up my own bed and net and bring up my canvas bath and chair. Finally, I dozed, only to be awakened by the sound of roosters crowing and dogs barking. Someone screamed and church bells rang out as dawn broke. I longed for the quiet of the bush away from this heat and turmoil.

As soon as the government offices were open, I went the rounds of the tall building looking for someone to help get me out of the filthy establishment where I was staying. I finally found a man to help me with my predicament. He located two vacant rooms in the rest house, the old barracks on the hill above town. The native clerk, whom I had seen the previous day, just couldn't be bothered with a mere woman.

Eight weeks remained before Jock's tour of duty would be over. I had decided to pay him a visit and see what the Gold Coast was like. There seemed to be no objections to my making the journey. I paid off trusty Amadu and the cook and stored the Ford and my extra belongings. Three days later I boarded the steamship from England. We were taken to shore in a tender. In no time, I was passed through customs. A government official's wife was not questioned.

I was taken by car to the rest house on a rise overlooking the sea. It was fairly cool and comfortable and run like a small hotel. In the morning, I went by lorry to an old fort on the coast. Formerly a Portuguese castle, it was currently used as a rest house, perched on a promontory with extensive views on all sides. Here I waited for Jock, who was expected that night. When he arrived, he was hot and sweaty from a hard day's work. My delight in seeing him is impossible to describe. Heat and humidity were forgotten in the days ahead. At long last we were together in the field. His work was in that coastal section and I camped with his retinue.

I also had time to explore on my own during the weeks ahead, learning how to search for diamonds in the gravels of the large streams. It was not as easy as gold panning, since the diamonds did not sink to the bottom of the diggings. They "flashed" through the pan like small twinkling stars amidst the quartz grains. Your eye had to be quick to spot them; if not, they disappeared.

In June, Jock and I returned to England. At Freetown the Ford and my goods from storage were loaded into the ship's hold. Miss Carey came aboard for luncheon. She hoped to return on leave soon. Among the returning passengers was Mr. Babcock from the Makong gold mine. He asked me to meet the chairman of his company back in London. To my surprise, I was offered a job with the Maroc Company to start when my husband returned to the Gold Coast in October. I was to prospect throughout the concession that they had been granted and look for new areas to mine. I would be searching the hills for the source of the gold in the gravels and exploring out in the bush. This was the life I loved. I felt confident that I knew the country, the ways of the natives, and how to choose carriers. I would not be stationed at the mine. There was no question of my refusing. Jock and I went on vacation knowing my plans for that fall and winter had already been decided.

There's Gold in Those Gravels

AFTER A SUMMER of rest and travel in England, Jock and I were ready to return to West Africa. I was to take up the job of prospecting for gold for Maroc, Ltd., in Sierra Leone. The company was sending out equipment with me to take to their mines. My goods were carefully divided into boxes with sufficient quantity of food to make me completely independent for weeks in the bush. I could take two boxes at a time, and send to the mine for others as I ran out.

The boat trip of eleven days was too short. Suddenly, the mountains of the lion appeared, clothed in mist, and we dropped anchor in Freetown harbor. After a hasty good-bye to Jock, I boarded a launch. In no time, I was in the heat and humidity of the crowded dock, surrounded by throngs of perspiring natives, pushing and shouting and calling out to the arrivals, demanding to be employed. A woman unescorted was fair game. I was mobbed, unable to hunt for my goods. The custom officials ignored me. Suddenly, out of the crowd, a small man pushed his way through. Amadu to my rescue!

How Amadu knew I was coming was a mystery. But there he was, spick and span, accompanied by a tall, domineering type of native. Amadu presented him and vouched, "He be proper cook for Missus" as he thrust some papers of recommendation in my hands. I was not about to argue and hired Lamina on the spot. The two quickly pushed back the mob and started to find all my pieces. Since there were forty items, it was an almost impossible job. The customs official said it would take several days to check them all. Each item had to be taxed. There might be a problem with some of the machinery and tools for the mine. There was nothing to do but go to the Mines Department for help.

In the office I found a telegram from London directing me to work at the Makong mine for the present. Later, I would go prospecting. Since Miss Carey was in England, I found a room in the rest house, where I "camped out" with the few things I managed to get through customs. The next days were spent securing the prospecting permit, clearing the mound of equipment through customs, and paying the taxes. I was able to shop for odds and ends I had not brought out from England.

At last the day came when I boarded the train for the trip to Magburaka. True to form, I arrived in a thunderstorm. Carriers were hastily engaged to carry my loads to the rest house. I was standing, bewildered, in the tropical downpour, wondering what to do, when an efficient, well-dressed native appeared, carrying a large umbrella. He had been sent from the Makong mine to meet me. He said he had a lorry to take me ten miles north to the rest house in Matotaka. He promised to take care of the loads and bring them later.

At the rest house in Matotaka I was met by Bai Kaferi, the paramount chief of the region, very impressive with his gold nose ring, gold distaff, flowing gown, and crown-like cap. He said he would return in the morning before I left for the Maroc gold mine.

At dawn everything was chaos. The headman had arrived with all of my goods which he was lining up in bundles of sixty or seventy pounds. Twenty carriers had appeared from the mine. They were busily choosing their loads for the twenty-mile trek to Makong. Several rushed to grab a small, two-foot-square box that looked easy to carry. As each one hefted it, they looked puzzled and dropped it, going for a larger load. The box was an iron container filled with mercury, and exceedingly heavy. Some of white man's juju, they guessed. No one would touch it.

By this time Chief Bai Kaferi had appeared to watch the scene. I asked for his help. He produced a stalwart fellow whom he instructed to shoulder the magic box. I also asked for two extra men to go with me, one to push my cyclometer wheel, which gave me distances up to a tenth of a mile, and the other to carry my sledgehammer, knapsack, compass, notebook, and lunch-box. One of them would also carry me across rivers.

At last we were off, just as the sun rose above the treetops and the mists began to lift from the valley. I caught up with the carriers in the first village, where they were drinking palm wine. I chided the headman for this lapse and told him to push the carriers on as fast as possible. It was four o'clock when I finally reached the Makong mine. I was completely exhausted. It takes time to adjust to the heat and humidity and I was not yet used to staying out in the sun all day. The two engineers at Makong, Wren and Parker, greeted me cordially and offered tea. A spacious mud house, newly whitewashed that day, had been built for my use.

Finally, the carriers struggled in with my loads. Amadu and Lamina sorted things out. When they finally had my bed and mosquito net set up, I told them to tackle the rest in the morning. Quickly I crawled into bed. It was still dark the next morning when

Workers at gold mine loading head pans to take to sluice box, Sierra Leone, ca. 1933

the loud bell rang to wake the laborers in their compound. Amadu appeared, sleepy eyed, with a cup of tea and a banana. Dressing hastily, I went out to greet the sea of faces lined up in front of the Makong buildings. Roll call was being held for the workers, who were assigned to their respective jobs in the placer workings.

Momo Beer, the headman assigned to me, helped me pick out a dozen eager, strong-looking men for my personal crew. My job was to find the source of gold in these placer deposits, if it was possible. I was to map the rocks of the area, taking samples to crush to see if they carried gold. I was also to look for quartz veins in the nearby hills to see if they contained gold. I would map the rocks beneath the placers as they became exposed.

The placer deposits were gravels laid down by streams from the neighboring hills. Any gold they carried was deposited in the bottom of the stream beds. To find the gold, trenches had to be made across the valleys. The water necessary to wash these gravels was brought in from distant streams in trenches or "leets," which had to be at contour level so it would flow downhill. The network of leets extended for several miles around the slopes. Since they often cut right through the soil, reaching the bedrock, they were excellent places to study the rocks. I could see that my work would take a long time. I wanted to get started.

Wren, the manager, was most helpful. He showed me how to cut samples from the pits dug in the gravels and test them for gold and how to pan the residue at the bottom of the pits and collect the specks of gold in a drop of mercury. The mercury was then boiled off in a spirit lamp and the gold weighed on a prospector's scale. I could then calculate the value of gold in the gravels per cubic yard.

At this time, the value of gold was not appreciated by the natives. On one occasion the manager put down a penny and a small gold nugget and offered his servant his choice. He picked the penny. One day when I was returning from a distant village, I met a messenger from the mine headed for the train to Freetown. On his head he carried four small gold bars worth ten thousand dollars. His only escort was an unarmed soldier. The insurance was less if the guard was unarmed. It was not long before things changed. As mining spread through the country, the natives demanded higher wages and stealing of the gold nuggets began.

I spent two months mapping the bedrock of the placer workings. My work gave the company a record of what lay under the piles of boulders and gravels that were being discarded. I had the men dig pits away from the workings to see if gold could be found. I also had them dig pits in the terraces of the smaller streams that entered the main river. While the pits were being dug, I took six men and their machetes with me to clear the bush so I could go up all the small streams to collect samples of the rocks.

Some of the quartz veins I found were disappointing. They carried very little gold. Others showed visible grains. I took samples of these veins and crushed them, testing for gold; many had positive results. I tried to find a pattern in the gold-bearing veins. They seemed to carry more gold near the contact of the schists and granite. But I was unable to locate any rich reefs. Later, as I moved north, I found gold associated with the iron ore beds that I had traced the previous year. Small quantities seemed to be scattered throughout the higher hills. I concluded that most of the gold placers had collected from the wearing down of the hills by erosion over long periods of time. The heavy gold concentrated in the gravels was deposited by the streams.

I found the work interesting but exhausting. I was used to the heat and humidity by now, but longed to go out on trek. The miners accepted me as one of their own. They had adopted animals for their amusement. Puppies, mongooses, and a chimpanzee — and even a caged leopard. When they sat up at night over their whiskeys and sodas, I collapsed in bed under my mosquito net and left them to their revelry.

The manager's delight was a young leopard, a nasty little beast whom no one could approach. I took pity on the poor thing tied to a log in front of our compound and pushed a box behind it as shelter from the sun. A daily meal of chicken was thrown in on a string. Spitting and snarling the leopard would grab the animal, take it into the box, and devour its meal. One night, when the men had consumed several bottles of whiskey, the manager, on a dare, said he could pet that damned cat. I had long since retired to bed and was awakened by much shouting and screaming. I grabbed my revolver and rushed outside to see what the uproar was about. By moonlight I could make out the manager struggling with the leopard, hanging on for dear life as the enraged beast clawed and bit him. It was impossible for me to take a shot. Finally, the manager's strong hands choked the leopard. We bathed his wounds with antiseptic and bound up the cuts on his arms. For several days he ran a fever but luckily survived. Later, when the wounds healed, he strolled through the village to show off his scars and to boast about how he had strangled a leopard with his bare hands.

When Christmas came, I felt I had finished my work at the mine. A few days later Mr. Babcock, who was now a director of the company, arrived from England with his wife. Things had slackened. The manager had gone off to the hospital in Freetown with some strange malady. Mr. Babcock soon had the paddocks humming with activity. Order and discipline ruled. The machine in the lower paddock, which had been abandoned for some weeks, was working. There was a new gasoline pump in the large flats so that work could begin there. Gold output suddenly shot up. The five engineers who came out with Mr. Babcock had been sent to start new placer mines in likely places to substitute for the placers that would soon be worked out.

Mr. Babcock went over the maps and reports I had made and decided I could go out to prospect new territory. I would first go north in the area where they had their concession and then further afield to unexplored areas. I was delighted. My loads were made up for a three months' supply. I would be able to live off the land in many areas where there was farming. Bread could be made from palm wine and flour. We could depend upon cassava root, which tastes like potato, and rice in the regions where it was the staple diet. There was a "cook's box," which contained a gallon tin for boiling water, various pots, pans, and cutlery necessary for cooking, and my lightweight plastic dishes. My large kettle was tied on top of this box. Each of the boxes must have weighed seventy to eighty pounds. One box had four five-gallon tins, one of which contained kerosene for the lamps. A second five-gallon tin held whatever the cook needed for everyday food, such as bananas and rice. On top of these were tied two empty five-gallon tins. These would be the cook's stove. He would build a fire in one and boil water on top of it and do his cooking. If he wanted to bake, he would place the other empty tin on top of his "stove" and use it as an oven.

I had an office box in a tin trunk that contained my books, maps, and instruments for weighing the gold. They were all carefully packed with clothes for protection. At the bottom, my cash box and revolver were hidden. Another tin trunk was filled with clothes and odds and ends I might need. There were two loads of picks, shovels, and head pans, plus machetes for each carrier. My tent made one load. My bed and bedding, canvas bath, a small table, a deck chair, and a small chair made up the bulkiest load of all.

I needed sixteen carriers plus someone to push my cyclometer wheel and carry my knapsack. Another was to carry the sledgehammer, compass, and notebook. He was to be with me at all times. The carriers had been carefully chosen by Momo Beer, who was to be my headman.

I was to go first to Matotaka, twenty miles away, to start work in Bai Kaferi's territory. To be sure every one would make the trip in one day, twenty were chosen to relieve my crew half way along the route. My retinue must have been a pretty sight as we filed out of the Makong compound early in the morning. Amadu had acquired a small helper who was to carry a precious lantern. Lamina also carried a lantern. Behind the caravan came several women, wives of the carriers. Two of them had babies tied on their backs. As we went north, we acquired more women. The men found wives cheaper in this area and spent their weekly wages for them. The men were more contented, I found, if they had their wives along to cook meals for them. It was lucky we had the extra retinue. Loads were dropped and some of the carriers took off to the bush. The heat and humidity, plus tsetse flies, made the going uncomfortable.

I reached Matotaka in the late afternoon well ahead of the carriers. Crowds of curious villagers followed me to the rest house. They had seen the "Gold Missus" before. A headman of the village greeted me and said that Bai Kaferi was ill. Since it was important for me to get his permission to prospect in his territory, I asked to see him. I was led to a small hut where he was in hiding. The chief lay on a raised mud bed in a small, windowless room. Covered with skins and blankets, he was very weak and his breathing was raspy. I suspected he had pneumonia. It was the custom to have the head of the current chief severed before his death and placed on the previous chief's body. Then his body would be buried to await the next chief's head. Thus precautions were used to secrete Bai Kaferi in case one of his enemies beheaded him before he died.

Bai Kaferi granted me permission to look for gold on his land. Since the neighboring chief at Makong had become rich from mining in his region, Bai Kaferi was anxious to have gold found on his land. He said he would send a guide with me to the hills, where his farms were located. He also gave me strong men to replace the carriers who had deserted. I am sure he looked forward to getting part of the shilling a day the laborers would earn.

The trials of getting started on trek began that evening. The carriers demanded that three pence for chop money be advanced to them. Four reported sick. I gave them some castor oil for "belly palaver." The one with a cut foot had to have it bathed in disinfectant and bandaged. My headman, Momo Beer, complained of a headache. I gave him some quinine.

The next morning at dawn, everything was chaos. The headman of the village appeared with the usual dash of a chicken, a few eggs, and a calabash of vegetables from Bai Kaferi to whom I sent back six shillings, which I hoped he got. When the loads were distributed with much argument, we finally took off. Two guides led me. I decided that James Conte, from the Makong mine, should be the one to carry my sledgehammer and knapsack. Since he could speak the language of this region, he turned out to be an invaluable helper. Momo Beer would bring up the rear and see that all went well.

After crossing a large stream and its wide terrace, we climbed steadily, finally reaching Bai Kaferi's farm in late afternoon. The farm was located high in the hills above a slight plateau. Here, the trees had been cut and burned and the crops planted between the charred logs. A small thatched hut was in the middle of the plantings where the "farmer" and his wives and children lived.

There was a stream not far away with a large floodplain. I decided to have my camp set up in the open clearing nearby. When the carriers struggled in, the routine of setting up camp began. Various men were assigned to jobs that they would continue to perform over the months ahead as we moved north. The tent had to be set up, the ridge pole put together, and the fly placed in proper position.

If I was in a camp for several days, a small projection or shelter was built at the entrance to my tent to act as a dining area. My deck chair, table, and "ruckee" chair were set up in its shade, and it would keep me dry in the daily torrential rains. A latrine was built, just a hole in the ground that could be filled in when we broke up camp. A small shelter was quickly constructed to act as a kitchen. My boxes were lined up under the fly. A trench had to be dug around the tent to drain off the rainwater. Water for camp was obtained in the empty five-gallon tins. Lamina and Amadu sent the men to get firewood. This routine would go on every time I moved camp. I was always surprised at how quickly the men learned to set it up. The sooner it was finished, the sooner they could "go for village" to chop and sleep.

There would be at least five days' work in the vicinity of Bai Kaferi's holdings. Each day I chose places where pits should be dug to collect samples of the gravel to test for gold. Then I took men to follow up the streambeds to study the rocks of the area. Upon my return in the afternoon, I took samples from the pits that reached "clay" or rock. The bottom foot of gravel and a few inches of clay were carefully washed in the gold pans. Momo Beer and I were the only ones to do the final "swishing." We examined the last few spoonfuls to see if there were any flecks or small nuggets of gold. I collected them in a small drop of mercury, which would be put in a test tube and carefully labeled. I then plotted the location of each pit on a map.

Once a week I wrote a report for the Maroc Company after I had dissolved the ball of mercury over a small spirit lamp, leaving the gold as a residue. This would then be carefully brushed on to the tiny tray of my prospector's weighing scales, so I could calculate the gold's worth. At that time, gold was worth $35 an ounce!

The maps I had were not always accurate. One day, after working along the height of land, I decided to follow the head of a stream shown on the map. It led to the main river in the valley near my camp. As we progressed downstream I noticed the compass bearing pointing in the wrong direction. It was late in the afternoon and there was no way to retrace our steps. As dusk approached, we reached a small village miles from camp. Since it was impossible to reach the camp before dark, we had to spend the night there.

The native headman was most solicitous. He produced a hammock for me, which was hung from a large cottonwood tree just outside the village. A watchman was provided. After an uncomfortable night, I was presented a row of eight poisonous snakes, neatly beheaded and lined up by the watchman's fire. It took us several hours to trek back to camp. Momo Beer and Amadu were relieved to see me return safely.

It was a week before I was ready to leave Bai Kaferi's land. I had found rich iron ore on the crest of the hills, an extension of the beds I had mapped to the north the previous year. But my message to Bai

Kaferi when we broke up camp and moved ten miles to the north was disappointing. I had not found any good prospects of gold. However, he did have a rich iron deposit on the top of the ridge. Since this site was only a hundred miles from the coast, it was possible that it could be mined at some future date. There might be a demand for iron overseas.

Week after week I moved north, making camp about ten miles distant in village after village. The men were happy with their work. They enjoyed the chance to meet some of their distant countrymen. They spread tall-tales about the Gold Missus who had very powerful juju and could find gold in the gravels and hills.

What kept me going through all the heat and humidity, the insect pests, and the unsuspected trials of camp life was the explorer's anticipation of a new adventure around each bend.

The chiefs and their dashes and the native customs fascinated me as well. I was as much of a curiosity to them as they were to me. We enjoyed "speaking" to each other in sign language when no interpreter was present. I learned so much.

After several discouraging weeks, I came into more promising county. The pits yielded gold in large enough quantities to collect samples. To reach the hills on the opposite side of the valley we had to cross a large river. We decided to camp at the base of the two-thousand-foot-high hills, where the floodplain was broad. We attempted to make pits but they all caved in as the groundwater level was high. By submerging, we could scoop up a handful of gravel in the gold pan. All the gravels retrieved contained some gold and even an occasional tiny nugget.

There were many small streams coming off from the hills, each producing gold in the pits where gravel from them spread out into the broad valley. I sent off a messenger to Mr. Babcock at the Makong mine, asking whether I should "peg" any prospects here. Mr. Babcock arranged to have the whole area included in an "exclusive prospecting lease." He said he would send out several engineers to make a detailed examination of the area to see if placer mines could be developed.

In the meantime, I had followed up stream after stream to see if I could locate any source of the gold. All around were boulders containing flecks of a shiny, steely-looking mineral. I took samples to take back to Freetown to be tested. They turned out to contain the rare mineral molybdenum, which had not been previously reported in Sierra Leone. Most of the world's output was mined at Climax, Colorado.

Mr. Babcock next ordered me north to Nerekoro, where their prospecting permits had been allowed to lapse. He had heard that some prospectors were in the vicinity. I was to peg any promising places and I had to hurry.

North of Nerekoro, along the Tonkolili River where I had met a prospector the previous year, I found another prospector only five hundred feet down stream from where I had planned to camp. I sent a messenger posthaste to Mr. Babcock, asking him to send me the mining laws and inquiring if I should jump a claim above where the prospector was working.

I had my camp set up on a plateau high above the Tonkolili River in orchard bush country with a large clearing made in the elephant grass. This location would be drier than near the river bottom. It was March and heavy storms were frequent in the evenings. The rainy season was approaching. Then I returned to the river bank and started to have the men make a pit. I hoped to be able to sample the bottom gravel.

Leaving Momo Beer in charge of the pitting, I went downstream to meet the prospector. He was pleased to see me, or so he said. He was using a drill to reach the bottom gravels. I knew he would encounter large boulders and never reach the gold-carrying sands. He said I could not possibly pit so close to the river. And when I went back to where Momo Beer and a crew were working, I found this to be true. As fast as they bailed water from their hole, more came in; the sides collapsed. We decided to make a larger pit and lined it with ten-foot-long logs tied together. Four men with head pans bailed out the water as fast as possible. This digging and bailing went on all day, but still they couldn't reach bottom. When we got down fifteen feet, I got a quick sample before the walls collapsed; it contained a few flecks of gold. It was hopeless to go on digging and we quit for the day. I sent a messenger to Makong to ask for a pump.

At supper that evening a runner arrived from Mr. Babcock, carrying the mining laws. He said to stake a claim immediately, regardless of my findings. Momo Beer and a few of my men went down to the river with me in the pouring rain. By the light of two lanterns, we cut posts. One was set up below my pit and the other a quarter of a mile upstream. Slipping and sliding in the dark, we tried to avoid falling into the swollen stream. Finally we had staked our claim. I felt rather guilty about "claim jumping" and I wondered what the prospector would think when he found our markers. He was actually very pleasant when he came to see me the next day and said he was returning to Freetown and giving up the idea of hunting for gold "in this godawful country."

After preparing maps and filling out the forms required by the Mines Department, I dispatched them with a messenger so they would make the next train to Freetown. I also sent Mr. Babcock a note saying I had staked the claim and telling of my plans to explore the neighboring hills in search of any source of gold until I heard from him further.

I spent the next few days making pits in the floodplains of the smaller streams in the area and exploring the heights above camp. Mr. Babcock and his wife decided to come to inspect the region. They arrived by hammock a few days later, using the wider trails along the main rivers. Their huge tent dwarfed mine. They traveled in style, with silverware and even candles for dining at night.

The next two days Mr. Babcock and I set out to see the pit by the river. He decided to send for two pumps and an engineer to bottom my pit. I had done all I could. The Mines Department inspector arrived two days later to inspect the claim. He, too, traveled by hammock. They marveled at my endurance. Frankly, I preferred walking to being carried.

The area to the north of Nerekoro had been closed to prospecting because of the iron ore deposits I had mapped the previous year. It was decided that I should explore the other side of the range. I could work south and head for Makong. My tour was about to end. The rains were beginning and it would be impossible to do work once they were on us.

To reach the other side of the range we had a tough climb of two thousand feet. From the top we had a good view. We could even see Bintimani, the highest peak in Sierra Leone, fifty miles to the north. My carriers grunted and groaned, but they were spurred on by the promise that we would be heading south, following the river valley, a sparsely settled area. White man was a rarity.

We moved camp almost every day, traveling twelve miles at the most. The men dug a few pits in the tributary gravels while I made a quick exploratory trek to the top of the range, going back to camp along small streams that drained from the heights. I hoped to get back to the Makong mine before the torrential rains, which were becoming more frequent.

As we neared Makong, the samples from our pits yielded more signs of gold. This area would be worth more extensive testing. It might prove possible to mine. Again we had to cross the range to reach the valley leading to Makong. As I walked those final long miles back into camp feeling hot, tired, and foot weary, I realized how lucky I was to have been in country untouched by the development that accompanied mining. The white man would come to get the best out of the land. Towns would grow up and the beautiful jungle would be devastated. The natives would abandon their customs and become greedy for money. "Civilization" would be a curse. I would cherish the memories I had of the days before such "progress."

The whitewashed mud huts of the Makong compound arrived only too soon. There was not a blade of grass in sight, just an open space cut out of the beautiful forest. Where the land had been stripped, devastation was everywhere. I paid off my carriers, who hated to see me leave. They would now have to return to hard labor in the paddocks. Amadu and Lamina would return with me to Freetown and care for my wants there until I sailed to England.

At Makong I wrote up reports and went over my maps with Mr. Babcock. I already missed the jungle life. Soon I was off to Mabonto on that long, hot trek to get the train to Freetown, where I was again entertained by Miss Carey. Amadu wept when I said good-bye. I was completely taken aback. Since he couldn't remember his own parents, I had apparently become a mother figure to him. There was nothing I could say to comfort him. I promised him that if I ever returned he could work for me again. I would always cherish his devotion and was sorry to leave him to a questionable future.

I waved good-bye from the launch I took out to the ship in the bay. Most of those on board were returning from tours of duty in West Africa, resting in the cool breezes and enjoying the comforts of civilization. As we rounded the "boneyard," a white shroud was quietly slipped overboard. The sea had claimed another victim of the tropics, dead from malaria.

Unfinished Business

ON RETURNING to London, I found a small flat and set up housekeeping. Jock would be back from the Gold Coast in six weeks. The days passed quickly. I found much to do in establishing a home where Jock and I could settle down for a short reunion. We both needed a rest and some time together. When he returned, we discussed my future. I knew I would not be content to spend a year alone in England; perhaps I could find my direction in Africa. The Maroc Company did not need a geologist or prospector any longer. I was tempted to go back to Sierra Leone and search for the source of the molybdenite I had found, but the company was interested only in gold. If I did return to Sierre Leone to complete my "unfinished business," I could proceed on my own into the mountains. Later I could travel to the Gold Coast to visit Jock. He was in full agreement with my plans.

With the year ahead in proper perspective, we enjoyed our short summer respite together. We spent the days resting and traveling. It was a pleasant homecoming, but our hearts were elsewhere.

In October we again set sail for West Africa, I to Sierra Leone and Jock to the Gold Coast and his work with the Geological Survey. When I left the ship and went ashore, I found that Freetown was now familiar territory. Hot and tired, I was struggling to clear my goods through customs when a smiling face appeared to my rescue: Amadu! Somehow he had heard of my arrival. Ever faithful, he was anxious to please and go on trek with me. Miss Carey entertained me as usual. She longed to go into the high country of the north. Since I had planned an extensive trip into the area of inselbergs, we arranged to meet at Christmas, a few day's trek north of Sefadu, in the eastern mountains near the border of Guinea. But first I planned to return to Magburaka and the area to the east to make an extensive search in the hills near the Mapoko River, where I had found specimens containing molybdenite. To be sure, the specimens were from boulders, but they had puzzled me. The Mines Department had sent them for analysis and found that they indeed contained molybdenum, not previously reported in this area. It was valuable for use as an alloy of steel. But unless found in large quantity, it would not be profitable to mine in Africa.

In the few short months I had been away many changes had taken place up country. Maroc had sent out engineers to some of the areas I had reported as showing good prospects of gold. They spent time testing these places to see if it would be worth starting placer mines. The natives had at last learned the value of gold. Crafty coast natives as well as Syrian traders were stealing at the sluice boxes.

When Amadu, a new cook I had hired, and I reached Magburaka, the chief greeted me cordially. He would help me pick out carriers and see me on my way. The trusty headman of my previous tour, James Conte, arrived like magic. He had heard of my arrival and had taken "Dutch leave" of the Makong mine. Two other seasoned carriers left the Marampa mine near Makeni. They too wanted to trek with the Gold Missus once more. With sixteen carriers and helpers, I set out.

Trekking into the interior, we reached the Mapoko River and followed its course into the hills. I chose a campsite in an open space, near where the river steepened. It was only a mile from a small village, so the carriers could be sheltered at night. I would stay alone with a night watchman, content not to be shut in by the forest.

I spent days making treks into the mountains, following all the tributaries within reach of my camp. Six natives proceeded ahead of me, clearing a way with machetes. Then, on reaching the end of the stream, I worked up to the height of land. After moving along the top, I picked up the head of another tributary stream that led down to the Mapoko or one of the larger streams of the area.

On one of my traverses I picked out a tributary shown on the map and decided to follow it down the mountain. I had reached the top of the ridge 1,500 feet in altitude above our campsite. Down we went through the thick forest until we reached a small stream. Slipping and sliding we continued, but it led us in a direction away from the camp. Once again my map had been wrong. I had dropped behind the carriers, who were setting too fast a pace, and I was resting on a log. The pan-carrier who followed me let out a sharp exclamation. I looked quickly; he was pointing upward with his chin. Following his gaze I could see nothing but green creepers and vines. But I could feel "snake" in his look. There it was, a gray-green snake entwined in the creeper, his leaf-like head pointing at me at eye level only a few feet away. I backed up slowly. The green mamba followed. Swaying and seeming not to move, his body appeared to stretch out. Twigs crackled in front of me and James Conte appeared, stealthily, a stick in one hand and machete at the ready. A blow across the creeper struck the snake on the back. James Conte then cut off its head to be sure it was dead and we proceeded at a slower pace.

It was getting late. My compass kept veering more and more in a direction away from our campsite. This stream would lead far down the river from where we should go. It was too late to turn back, so we continued on until we came to a small farm that James Conte recognized. We had been there the previous year. We were miles from camp, but at least we knew where we were. Changing direction, at dusk we reached a small village, where we purchased oranges and bananas. Our choice was to wait here or go on in the dark. I was not anxious to repeat the experience of the previous year when I had spent the night near this same village, sleeping in a hammock under a large tree with no mosquito net. We had a hasty conference and decided to head for camp. My head pan was filled with burning embers to light the rough trail. The men could pick the way. The light of the moon also helped to guide us.

A few days later, while following a small stream, I came to a junction. Here, at last, was what I was looking for — a vein in which the shiny molybdenite was visible. We broke off large chunks to see more of the mineral. This was the place from which the boulders had come. Searching the area, I could find no other veins. It was time to continue on.

Going north, I circled around Lake Sonfon, where three men from the Maroc Company were already making pits, hoping to develop a mine. I calculated that I had to trek 165 miles in eleven days to reach my rendezvous with Miss Carey at Christmas at Sankan Birua, the high plateau north of Sefadu. The country I was approaching was high and dry, very much like Arizona. I felt up to the effort. I would not be doing prospecting on the way to delay me. I would travel with eleven carriers and make only one detour. At only a few hundred feet higher than Mount Washington in New Hampshire, Bintimani beckoned.

The chief in the village at the base of Bintimani provided me with a guide. Since the mountain could not be climbed in one day, I planned to camp half way to the summit. I decided to take as few carriers as possible and sleep out in the open. I sent the tent and heavy boxes with Amadu around to the opposite side of the mountain to meet me on our descent.

We got an early start and climbed through the morning mist. Leaving orchard bush country, we came into a cool mahogany forest. About eleven o'clock we reached a place near a brook where we would camp for the night. There was no trail beyond. I had seen large, circular holes, at least a foot across, in the mud of the forest. The guide explained they were elephant tracks made the previous day, after a heavy thunderstorm. I left a man to tell the carriers to make camp here and await our return in the late afternoon.

We plodded ahead and suddenly came into the orchard bush. High above I could see the rounded peak of Bintimani, "the old man of the mountain," the interpreter translated. "A devil lives there." I decided to call it "Devil's Mountain." The climbing became steeper but there were no cliffs in sight as we came into high elephant grass, which became shorter and shorter, and finally completely disappeared. We were surrounded by bare boulders. One last scramble and we had reached the top. I had hoped for a wide view of the surrounding country, but the blue harmattan haze had closed in, completely hiding the valley in every direction. Other inselbergs surrounded us, rising above the mists.

Eating a belated lunch of bananas, oranges, and biscuits, we rested in the shade of boulders. The guide produced a tin can said to be left by the devil. He instructed me to sign my name on a paper, which listed several other visitors who had made the climb. A "toll" had to be paid to the devil to appease him; otherwise, bad luck would befall me. I refused to fall into this trap.

As we returned through the slippery grass, we slid on our feet, grabbing handfuls of tall grass to check our speed. The men's bare feet were more effective in checking their speed than my worn hobnailed boots. At the edge of the orchard bush, the guide stopped in alarm. There below us was a whole herd of the dangerous "bush cow," the native buffalo. Luckily, we were downwind, so they hadn't spotted us. Then suddenly the leader raised his head. He had seen us. He snorted, turned, and dashed down into the orchard bush. The whole herd turned to follow. We waited until they were out of sight before proceeding.

Just as dusk descended, we came to our camp. Amadu had forgotten to put matches in the chop box so a swift-footed native was sent back down the path to a farmer's hut. He returned with a firebrand as darkness closed in. After a hasty meal, I crawled into my bed. It had suddenly grown cold, so there was no need for a mosquito net. The men spent a miserable night crowded around their small fire. The wind whistled through the tall mahogany trees. It was the coldest night I had experienced in Sierra Leone.

After reaching our carriers, we pushed ahead, fifteen miles a day. The chiefs in this area had cows and horses since we were out of the tsetse-fly belt. One chief rode ahead on his horse to meet me, followed by a small boy, who carried the saddle on his head. The villagers followed with drums and bean-shakers. The chief presented me with a cow for which I dashed him ten shillings in return. I gave the animal to my men, who had a feast in the village that night.

Within a day's march of my goal to the heights of Sankan Birua, another chief presented me with a bleating sheep, which I accepted. It would be excellent chop at Christmas. But the lamb refused to budge. The boy who brought the animal swung it around his neck holding the feet in front, with the head dangling, and then joined our group. This cruelty troubled me deeply, but it was the custom of the country.

At last we reached the steep path that led to the 4,000-foot plateau of Sankan Birua. We climbed through the cool of a mahogany forest and came to a gully of feathery tree ferns, the first I had seen in the country. Next came the orchard bush, and finally the elephant grass. The top of the plateau was covered with a much shorter grass. Above the plateau we could see the top of Sankan Birua, a high, rounded peak of granite.

Two rest houses had been built on the plateau, one made of grass, the other of mud. Each had two rooms. A central open-sided bari lay between them. The D.C. at Sefadu had told me two years before that this was the most healthy place in the protectorate. The white people of Sierra Leone came here for vacations to recover from the hot, humid areas of the south. Freetown had 190 inches of rain a year. No one came at this time of year, however. The harmattan blew every day from noon to midnight and it was bitterly cold after dark. The haze at this time of year obstructed the view from the plateau. Miss Carey arrived a day later, traveling by hammock from Sefadu. We were joined the next day by one of Miss Carey's colleagues, who had decided to meet her to spend Christmas with us on the high plateau.

Our Christmas was strange. The harmattan howled as we sat snug inside the grass hut eating some delicacies cooked from the sheep we had brought. Despite the bitter wind, we stayed for a week, climbing several of the peaks around us, including Sankan Birua. We rose at dawn to return by noon before the harmattan winds became violent. The summits were all granite, rounded and easy to climb. The views were disappointing for the haze obscured everything below.

Returning to Sefadu, we spent the night at the village below the summit of the plateau, where we found a comfortable rest house. Next day we trekked the long march to Sefadu, to spend New Year's with Brown, the D.C. whom I had met two years before in Kenema when my Ford had to be rescued from the flatcar. Then Miss Carey returned to Freetown while I took a short trip by lorry to visit the recently opened diamond mines, which were now booming.

At the diamond fields I found great activity. Placer mining was in progress. A large floodplain of river gravels was being destroyed. The gravels were worked over and dumped into sluice boxes. The end "tailings" were collected and sorted by hand. Sheds had been built where native girls worked over the fine gravels, picking out the small diamonds as they flashed for a second, obtruding from the grains of sand.

In Freetown I paid off my cook and Amadu and retrieved my loads, which had arrived ahead of me. I then waited for the boat to the Gold Coast, where I would meet Jock and travel about that country. Amadu was tearful and I found it equally hard to part with him. He wanted to go with me. Although I was tempted, I feared he would not get along with the natives of the Gold Coast with whom I would be trekking. He hoped to be a "proper servant boy" for some other master. I wrote him a letter of recommendation. Having been trained by a missus, he could find jobs more easily than those who were taught by a white man.

The Gold Coast

A T L A S T I was on the boat headed for the Gold Coast, where I joined Jock for a short time before visiting the mines. It was a happy reunion, but I didn't want to interfere with his work. I planned to visit the mines to gather as much knowledge as I could which I would then use to explore in other parts of West Africa.

After spending a few days with Jock where he was camped, I visited a gold mine at Prestea, a long distance inland from the coast. Here, a rich vein of quartz-bearing gold had widened at depth. An enormous chamber, as big as a small house, had been excavated. All of it was rich in ore.

Nearer the coast at Tarkwa, I found a different sort of mine. The miners had followed a belt of conglomerate pebbles imbedded in sandstone, which had been transformed into rock by heat and pressure. This type of deposit was similar to the rich and deep mines of Johannesburg in South Africa.

I also visited the placer diamond workings near the coast. Then I trekked to several remote areas to study the rocks, taking natives to clear the way with machetes to reach the outcrops. The underbrush and bushes were similar to those in Sierra Leone so I was used to our slow progress.

I had heard about a lake with a puzzling history and trekked in to see it at the bottom of what appeared to be a crater, like Crater Lake in Oregon, or perhaps Meteor Crater in Arizona. I camped near the bottom in a large cocoa plantation, where sand flies attacked us relentlessly, day and night. The lake was considered sacred; no boats were allowed. The fishermen caught their fish in nets that they cast from the shore. Circling the lake after a miserable night, I climbed to the rim on the opposite side to stay in a comfortable rest house used by white people as a vacation spot. It was deep in the forest and gardens of brilliant flowers surrounded the open area. One could sit outside and enjoy the view across the circular rim, with the lake glistening below.

I was still baffled by the origin of this large hole. There were no signs of volcanic activity: no lava flows in the sides. If it had been caused by a meteor, signs of the explosion had long since disappeared in the deep soils of the tropics. The forest that covered the slopes concealed any outcrops.

Showing off horned cerastes, Gold Coast, 1933

It was time to end my wanderings. The rains were due soon and the heat and humidity were oppressive. I went to Takoradi to meet a friend on the boat heading for Nigeria. Mary, the wife of the head of the Geological Survey of Nigeria, had invited me to join her and spend a few weeks touring that vast country. After saying good-bye to Jock and packing up my tent and other supplies, I took a lorry to Takoradi.

Swinging in a Bucket

A T TAKORADI I waited for the boat for Nigeria. Two days later it appeared. Mary was delighted to greet me. She feared I might not come. Off we sailed, enjoying two days of relaxation in the cool of the ocean. As we approached the coast of Nigeria, the boat threaded its way along a lagoon and tied up at the dock of Lagos, a real city. Everything was new and modern, with rows of well-built houses and a business area with buildings rising several stories high. It was not a bit like the other West African cities I had visited. This was a rich and prosperous country.

A man from the bank, who had been sent to take care of us during our short stay in Lagos, arrived soon after we docked. He ushered us ashore, drove us to his house, and entertained us royally. Before we boarded our train, he gave a dinner party. One of the waiters, in his starched white coat with rows of shiny brass buttons, stood silently behind my chair. It was Amadu! His ambition achieved, he was a proper servant at last. The banker had hired him in Freetown. My letter of recommendation had gotten him the job. Now he was traveling the rounds from country to country along the west coast of Africa as his boss visited the various branches of his English firm.

The night sleeper going north was comfortable, and despite the heat, we slept soundly. At noon the next day we crossed the Niger River, and leaving the forests, our train began to rise slowly to a low plateau country. Suddenly clouds of locusts descended on the countryside, covering everything in sight as they devoured the grass and leaves. The rails became slippery with the slime of their bodies. The engine stalled, then slid backwards. Puffing and snorting, it just couldn't make headway. Finally, after everything was eaten and the green of the countryside became a dark brown, we moved on.

At three in the morning we debarked at Kaduna Junction, where Mary's husband met us and drove us to their home, a lovely stucco house set amidst beautiful gardens. Exhausted, we slept late. Then came a series of visitors anxious to hear about the outside world. There was a round of parties every day for this was a large settlement of officials out on government business. Many had their wives with them. It was a healthy climate where they could live much as in England, but in far better circumstances. They had beautiful houses and native servants to tend to their every need.

I was able to escape this life of "high society" and went to visit the tin mines at Jos, a day's drive away. Here, placer mining was being done on a huge scale. Large machines were ripping up a wide valley, leaving destruction behind. The source of the tin had not been discovered. I had a few days to hike with an American geologist, who was searching the hills for tin deposits.

I had heard about a group of natives living several miles from Jos who were isolated from all the pressures of progress. They had never been converted by missionaries and lived as they must have in the past. Theirs was one of the oldest civilizations in West Africa. I made a trip to see these "pagans" and found them shy but friendly. They were just as interested in seeing a white woman as I was in seeing them. They were stark naked. The men carried bows and arrows to shoot game, their staple food, together with roots and fruits of the semi-jungle in which they were hidden from the world. They had built small thatched huts as living quarters, with a few burning logs in front on which to cook. They seemed happy and healthy. I wondered how long they could remain this way before mining or "progress" arrived.

On returning to Kaduna, I was approached by an army captain who had heard of my work prospecting for gold. He had a small gold prospect further to the north near Kano on the edge of the desert. He carried samples of gold from a vein and had started to have it followed to see if he could develop a gold mine. He asked me if I would make a report for him when I visited Kano. He would pay all my expenses in addition to a generous stipend. Needless to say, I accepted his offer.

Kano was an Arab city, ruled by a sultan king, at the end of the railroad, just south of the Sahara Desert. Great thick walls of mud encircled the city with a gateway through. Inside were narrow streets with large buildings on every side, topped by flat roofs with turrets. The occupants used these as we do piazzas, to get the evening breezes. Crowding the streets were monkeys, goats, and camels, amidst throngs of native Arabs clothed in white gowns.

I had been staying outside the city with the D.C. of the area. He sent me off to see the sights with an armed guard as it was not safe for a white woman to go about alone. The Arab women were swathed in colorful gowns, their faces concealed in their hoods. They would not understand a woman who was dressed like a man.

A day later I went to study the mine. It turned out to be only a deep hole, sunk fifty feet into the ground. For two days the native crew had been pumping water out of this "well." I had to descend in a bucket to see where the vein of ore was found. At the bottom I was to follow small tunnels in search of the veins of gold. Never before had I had a ride like this. A pulley lowered me in a bucket down into the shaft. I spun round and round to the bottom. Water was seeping in through the cracks of the granite, coming in as fast as it was pumped out. Gingerly I followed a side tunnel, narrow and airless; small veins of quartz appeared at the "face" of this opening. I hastily chipped out a few samples, then retreated to the circular opening and signaled to be hoisted up. The pumps ceased immediately as I came to the surface and I watched in fascination as that fifty-foot hole filled up below me. They had obviously not been able to find any large vein carrying gold. Searching the exposures of rocks at the surface, I learned why. There was a break in the quartz vein that yielded gold. It was offset for several feet and sloped away from the vertical. They had mistakenly sunk the pit where the large vein would not be found. There were only those little offshoots in the shaft, which would be worthless to mine.

After submitting my report to the captain, it was time to return to England. Jock would return shortly. We were both in need of a long vacation away from the debilitating heat of the tropics. The English always reminded us of the saying: "Only mad dogs and Englishmen go out in the midday sun."

I returned by train to Lagos and embarked on the ship for England. Two days later we stopped at Takoradi on the Gold Coast. As the boat docked, whom should I see on the dock but Jock with all his luggage, ready to go back to England. He had been stricken with malaria, so his boss decided to send him back early upon learning that Jock's wife would be on the ship headed for home. The twelve days on the ship were like a second honeymoon. We reveled in the luxury of our cabin and the sea breezes on deck. At night we watched the sunset and the moonrise. It was a chance to renew our life together without the hardships of bush life.

Back in the U.S.A.

I N L O N D O N we came to a decision. Jock was in need of an extended vacation. For years, since his teens, he had led a life of stress. First, had come the Gallipoli Campaign, where he was twice cited for bravery before being hospitalized with dysentery and malaria. Then he and some friends had decided to join the air force, preferring this to life in the trenches of France. After ninety-eight sorties in his own army bomber, he had collapsed. After the war, he went back to his studies, earning his Ph.D. in geology at Edinburgh University. The five years in Africa had taken their toll. We decided to go to America for a couple of years to restore Jock's health.

After our arrival in the States we traveled, spending winters in different university towns. I had hopes that Jock might find his "niche" in this country, where my roots were deep. I realized that our marriage could not survive repeated separations. I also wanted to help Jock with his fieldwork in Africa. I had proven myself capable during the three years there on my own. But the British Colonial Office remained adamant. They would not allow a geologist to take his wife to Africa and subject her to the hardships that his work would entail. Life on my own in the heat and humidity of the tropics no longer appealed to me.

Gradually I found myself becoming intrigued by the fieldwork being done in my native New Hampshire. A group of Harvard students, supervised by Marland Billings, a professor of geology at Harvard, were mapping the geology of the state. Then I found an opportunity to teach at Wellesley College, and Louise Kingsley, one of the geology professors there, decided to work with me in mapping the Cardigan Quadrangle in New Hampshire.

Despite the allure of America's national parks, Jock was anxious to go back. His place was not in America. He decided to return to England and his work in West Africa. I could not face returning to a dreary existence in London while waiting for him to return from his trips to the Gold Coast.

It tore me apart to say good-bye to Jock as he boarded the ship in New York. Perhaps it would be a trial separation, I thought. He was free to pursue his career in Africa. He was also relieved to see me established. As I became engrossed in my fieldwork in New Hampshire, we drew even further apart. Hard as it was to resolve our feelings, the marriage ties were severed. We parted, sad to face the fact that we could not work out our lives together.

After Jock returned to England, I took up teaching at Wellesley and spent the summer doing fieldwork in New Hampshire, fitting together the pieces of the state's geological jigsaw puzzle. Professor Billings was in charge of unraveling the secrets of the little-known rocks of the state. He assigned various "blocks" or quadrangles to his students to map for their theses, thereby constructing a geological map of the state.

Louise and I worked for two summers in the field to map the Cardigan region. We did the laboratory research in the winters, studying thin sections of rock samples. Teaching students took up much of our time. I found I loved the work and had a good rapport with the students. One of them, who was in my advanced course, admitted to me years later that when the subject seemed boring they would somehow manipulate the discussion back to my work in Africa to break the monotony.

To satisfy my friends who wanted to know about my life in West Africa, I wrote a book on my African experiences entitled *The Gold Missus, A Woman Prospector in Sierra Leone*. It was published in 1938 in the United States by W. W. Norton, but is no longer available. The British edition never got to the market, the proofs having been destroyed during the "blitz," when the publishing houses in that section of London were bombed and burned. The reminiscences I have included here are an abbreviated account of that book.

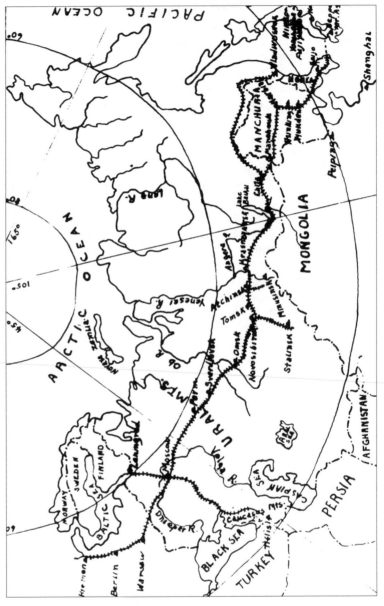

Route through Soviet Union, 1937

From the Kremlin to the Caucasus

URING THE SUMMER OF 1937, there was to be a geological congress in Russia. I couldn't resist the chance to learn firsthand about a section of the world I had long puzzled over. I seized the opportunity.

Shortly after my arrival in Moscow, I received a formal invitation for a banquet at the Kremlin, which was closed to the public in those days. The 75 x 300 ft. grand banquet hall was ablaze with candles, a total of 3,500 in the crystal chandeliers, according to a statistician friend. One hundred tables, seating twelve persons each, were covered with white tablecloths, each graced by twenty-one bottles of wine. Twenty-three courses were served by uniformed waiters; it took two and a half hours before the entrée. Between each course, some dignitary stalked down the length of the hall to the speaker's platform and delivered a speech, which was translated into English. I remember the names of Litvinov and Molotov. I hoped Stalin would appear. I learned later it was the night he purged thirty-five of his top army officers, shot without benefit of a trial.

As toasts were drunk to each of the dignitaries, I was feeling thirsty and spied a carafe of clear liquid. Eyes were turned toward me as I filled a crystal goblet and took a big swig of what I thought was water. It was vodka! As each dignitary passed, everyone rose to toast him. To my embarrassment, the Russian engineer on my right hoisted me bodily upon the table, so I could see better. He was getting quite drunk. He spoke good English, but was becoming obnoxious, insisting that I go home to his apartment after the feast. He pointed out how I could recognize the OGPU or secret police, two of whom were at our table. He observed that they wore black-banded wristwatches and that their clothes had a special cut. I began to get worried. I spotted a geologist from Princeton two tables away. Although he was a stranger, I scribbled a note and managed to have it slipped to him. In it I asked his help as escort back to my hotel. Finally, at three in the morning, he slipped over beside me. Two OGPU stood next to my engineer, who was being detained. As we walked back along a lighted brickway, my Princeton escort thought we should look at the huge Kremlin bell, a well-known reminder of days long past. Two armed guards stepped out from behind and motioned us on.

Our trip included a visit to Leningrad (Saint Petersburg) and its
museums. Buses were provided, with English-speaking "Intourist"
guides. We knew all about the woolly mammoth, housed there in the
natural history museum, but it was not on the schedule. Our busload
insisted, rebelling and refusing to get out at the next museum. We
would not obey orders until we saw the beast. We won. As it turned
out, the woolly mammoth was not woolly but rather an ugly plaster
replica, sitting on his haunches in a glass cage. Rows and rows of bottles stood in bookcases behind him. All his entrails had been preserved in formaldehyde. Even bottles of fur. The geologists were
convulsed with laughter at the stark naked replica. The Russians had
no sense of humor. They were grim and angry at our group for forc-
ing them to change the schedule.

We were also bused to communes in the country to see the peas-
ants in the field. They were very poor. In those days laborers earned
150–500 rubles per month depending upon the type of work.
Factory workers earned more. A professor got the highest salary,
2,500–10,000 rubles a month. A ruble was worth 20 cents.

We visited several schools in the country, as well as day-care centers for babies and toddlers, whose mothers and fathers all worked.
Potatoes and cucumbers provided the staple diet. They had no milk
in those days. The cattle had all been killed during the revolution
and war.

Wherever we traveled by train, we were met by crowds of curious
villagers. Statues of Stalin stood in prominent places with large signs
written in Russian and English posted below them: "Science is called
science just because it recognizes no fetishes, and does not fear to
raise its hand against everything that is obsolete and dying, and
attentively listens to the voice of experience and practice!"

Russia in 1937 was in turmoil. Stalin was establishing his iron hold
on the country. We were watched at every turn. Everyone was suspicious of the other. All the resident American engineers who had
helped establish the mines and factories were being sent back to the
United States. I was getting a bit nervous about going on a horseback
trip in the Caucasus Mountains and asked Mr. Davies, the American
ambassador, if it was safe to go. He said that anything the Russians
planned would be well supervised and we would have a chance to see
things that he had been refused. "Go! By all means," he replied.

I joined the large group of foreigners who started out by train
from Moscow for the Georgian Military Highway. First, we had baths

Women workers, Tiflis (Tbilisi), Georgia, 1937

in the mineral waters of Pyatigorsk, north of the highway. Each person was assigned to a cubicle with a white-clad woman attendant whose job was to scrub each of the members of the party. I heard several vociferous objections in various languages by the men, who were aghast at being scrubbed by females. Next we were taken into buses to cross the highway. We had been told that for security reasons no photographs were allowed within 150 yards of the roads. This rule was maintained throughout the country. No photographs from planes or pictures of army personnel. I am not sure whether I disobeyed this rule, but I was obviously picked out as suspect. I found

Kay (center) on "preliminary" horseback trip in Georgia (Soviet Union), 1937

myself assigned a "watchful" Russian companion, who was evasive in answering some of my questions.

We had a long day's drive through Georgia, arriving late in Tiflis (Tbilisi). Here, the group split up. Most of them planned to go on to Armenia. In addition, a busload of Russians and foreign geologists was to visit some manganese mines followed by a "preliminary" horseback trek southwest of the Georgian Military Highway. This was the trip I hoped to take for it was our testing-ground, used to weed out those unsuited for the trek across the western end of the Caucasus Mountains.

Dawn had us mounting on local horses commandeered from farmers, who rode with us for two days into the foothills of snow-covered mountains. The horses had been out in the rain all night and the saddles, which were made partly of straw, were soaked. They oozed on mounting and our clothes soon became stained a dark-brown color. I found myself walking a good part of the day to dry myself out and to try to dry the saddle.

As we approached higher ground, lunch was served at a small schoolhouse in a remote village, where we were introduced, or shall I say subjected, to the first of our ever-changing and unexpected sanitary facilities. We were to use a small bottomless outhouse hanging over the pigpen. Enough said! Primitive conditions were encountered everywhere in our travels away from the towns. But this one took the prize.

We did not reach our destination until midnight. It was a lovely chalet high in the mountains, where we were served a sumptuous meal. I regretted not being able to get good views of the scenery. The clouds hung low and it started to drizzle as we ventured out in the early morning for another fifteen-hour day. Several members of the party decided a week's horseback trip across the mountains was not their way to see the geology of the Caucasus. Some others had come down with intestinal illnesses and returned to Moscow. It was a tired group the next day when we reached a wine factory for lunch where there was nothing to drink but wine. We had already learned to avoid water of any kind and had to watch what we ate as dysentery was an ever-present threat.

The next lap of our trip was by train. Traveling west, we followed close to the Black Sea and then continued on by bus along the coast until we got to a town called Gagra, the starting point for the Caucasus trip. The evening after the preliminary horseback trip I awoke with cramps and nausea and spent most of the night in the lavatory of the train. The next morning I was so weak I could barely walk. I thought that this was the end of the Caucasus trip for me. Buses met our horseback group and drove us to a scientific station. We were always being sidetracked to see these cultural or educational facilities along our route. When the bus stopped, I simply folded up on the grass, abandoned by the rest of the group, who went on to be indoctrinated in the "progressive" methods of science.

I think I must have been hallucinating when I saw cages of snakes lined up in a row below the building. Soon a small retinue of white-clad men and women arrived, one of whom approached with a vicious-looking syringe filled with yellow fluid. A woman took my arm and started to plunge in the needle. I pulled back and said "Nyet! Nyet!" They remonstrated in words I couldn't understand. Where was the interpreter? My first thought had been that this was an experimental institute studying snake serum. I was not about to be injected with something I was allergic to. They finally gave up, not understanding my refusal of something they thought would help revive me. When the others returned an hour later, I was feeling slightly better.

Our next stop was for lunch, a grand spread along the banks of a river in a small village. Again I dropped down on the bank and refused food. I listened to the customary speeches of "guests" and village dignitaries. When we were about to leave, I was greeted by the Russian doctor of our party, who had completely ignored me when I had collapsed. He said that a special car had been provided for him.

He too had been taken ill. I was to accompany him. The rest of the day was a haze. I was glad to be ushered into a single room at the sea-side resort of Sukhumi on the Black Sea, where we spent the night.

The doctor was feeling worse the next day, so he got permission for us to travel ahead to where we were to start the horseback trip. We stopped for lunch at a lovely mosque, which had been converted into a hospital. Before being led to a small room with a cot, I had to admire the lovely paintings in the main room of worship, which was now in use as an operating theatre. Everything seemed to be very sanitary and professionally set up, except the "rest room," which turned out to be a lavatory room with a small stream flowing down the middle. To relieve myself I had to straddle this rivulet, supported by two attendants.

After a few hours of rest, we were on our way. The doctor explained that I would be allowed to go on the horseback trip the next day only if there was a stretcher and a doctor along. I resigned myself. A stretcher? That would be impossible.

Late in the afternoon, after climbing into the hills on rough roads, we came to a large chalet, several stories high, located in a forest of spruce and fir. Mountains rose behind it. I was led to a small room and told to rest. The doctor had disappeared. After an hour's sleep, feeling much refreshed, I got dressed and decided to explore. I entered a large room where several army men were sitting around, joking and drinking. My appearance caused consternation. Finally, one of the men, who spoke German, was able to converse. He was surprised to find an American in their midst and explained that this had been a hunting lodge of the czars and was now used as a rest home for "commanders" on vacation. In my poor German I was unable to explain who I was. Suddenly the doctor appeared and whisked me back to my room, with stern commands not to leave it again until he came for me. The rest of our party arrived after dark and we had a late meal. I could eat very little. The army commanders had all disappeared.

At dawn the doctor came to my room and informed me that I could go on the trip. There would be three stretchers as well as two doctors. My spirits rose. We were ushered out behind the barns to find a milling mass of horses and soldiers, which turned out to be a battalion of the Red Army. They were to be our escort. No wonder there were stretchers and doctors. They quickly shouldered our duf-fel bags and took them off to load on the packhorses. The head com-mander (no one was entitled to a higher rank although it was obvious who the head officer of the group was) looked over our party —

twelve foreigners and an equal number of Russians to accompany us. He then began to assign us horses. Mine was named "Anarhist" (Anarchist) and looked like a sturdy, but lively horse. A woman by the name of Helen was to be my guardian, interpreter, and watch-dog. We soon became fast friends, and she confided in me when others were not listening. Everywhere we went we were watched, and in turn, our watchers were watched. No one was to be trusted.

To my consternation, when I had packed that morning, my Leica camera was missing. I was assured by our leader that it would turn up. Nothing was ever stolen in Russia, he explained. I believed it had been deliberately "removed" somewhere along the trip the previous day. I was probably suspect for I must have taken some "illegal" photographs. To have me take pictures of the trip we were about to go on was unthinkable. The camera was never "found." Instead, I had to rely on generous friends for pictures of the places we visited. As we progressed, I realized that no photographs of soldiers were permitted. It became clear that this was a forced march to test our escort battalion.

After much shouting and milling around, we set off single file up a rough trail. This part of the czars' hunting grounds had never been deforested. We reveled in the smell of firs and spruce as we climbed higher. I was feeling better by the hour. Now I knew I could make the trip without having to be carried. By noon the forest gave way to shrubs and rhododendron bushes. They were glorious among the smaller brush. After a four-hour ride, we came out to tree line. The snow-covered peaks of the Caucasus rose on both sides as we approached a pass. After a quick lunch of bread and cheese, with a bottle of mineral water for me and wine for the others, we were on our way again. The going was slow. My arms were giving out trying to keep Anarchist in line. As the days progressed, Anarchist still insisted upon being up front. I began to realize that the commander had given him to me on purpose, to test this female geologist. I still believe that he was the commander's horse and therefore insisted upon being in the lead.

Since the purpose of this trip was to study the structure and rock sequence of the Caucasus Range, the group stopped periodically to look at outcrops. On the first day dusk found us high up on a plateau with no idea of when we would stop. The packhorses had not been seen since the start, and we wondered what we would do if night caught us. Coming over a rise, we looked down to see a row of white tents and smoke rising near three large tables. This camp had been set up by the battalion. Helen and I were assigned to one of the tents, where we found two cots made up with new sheets and blankets, all the comforts of home, things least expected in these mountains. It did not matter that the packhorses didn't arrive that night. Twenty-one kilometers was too much for them. We even found a separate wooden outhouse constructed for Helen, a Russian woman geologist, and me. Unexpected privacy and attention to sanitation on camping trips was indeed a surprise.

Supper of hot borscht and meat and vegetables was produced in no time by the army cooks, who had been left here to care for the camp. Breakfast was an unheard-of luxury: caviar and sour cream by the bowlful, ravenously consumed by the Russians. I opted for "manna-kasha," similar to cream of wheat. It was made especially on doctor's orders; only children or the sick or elderly were allowed this dish and I learned to ask for it on all occasions. The food at the camps was the cleanest and best prepared of any we had all that summer. The air at 8,000 feet was invigorating. There were no flies and we had lots of exercise. Before long I was a new woman. We took side trips to study the geology that first day out of camp. By evening the packhorses arrived with our duffel bags. We could finally change into fresh clothes.

I think it was on the third day that I just missed ending it all. We were moving camp and had to cross a large stream over which the army had built a suspension bridge on their way to the hunting lodge. Of course the commander led the way. His horse gingerly walked across, with Anarchist following close on his heels, despite my efforts to hold him back. With one lurch, Anarchist took the bit in his mouth and broke into a fast trot as we crossed the swaying bridge. I tugged with all my might and tried not to look down twenty feet below to the rushing stream. Across we went, no protection at the sides, just "guide rails." The bridge held and Anarchist stopped at the side of the commander, who rather grudgingly said, "You are a brave woman."

Next day I was assigned to the slow nag, Yermak. I would lag along way behind the others, hoping I would reach the next outcrop before the geologists moved on. To go up a steep slope, I dismounted. Grabbing Yermak's tail, I urged him ahead, dodging the pebbles he kicked up. The army horses had been trained to pull their mounts in this way. At least it broke the routine of riding.

On our last day before reaching camp, I was behind as usual. We had been descending to reach the north side of that part of the Caucasus. We were not allowed to let our horses drink until evening and Yermak was thirsty. I was walking behind him when he spotted the stream in the valley below, where he decided to quench his thirst.

He started straight down the steep embankment; instinctively I grabbed his tail and dug in my feet. I didn't know if I could hold him. Suddenly, out of the blue, a soldier came to my rescue. I had repeatedly seen foot soldiers scattered along the route, but I hadn't realized one had been assigned to me to see that I was safe. Together, we pulled Yermak back on the trail and walked side by side for the next mile. To my amazement he spoke good English and we had one of the most informative discussions I enjoyed with a Russian all that summer. As we approached the open glade in the forest where the others were already camped, he hung back and said he had to leave. No OGPU had interrupted our conversation and he wasn't anxious to be seen talking to me.

The camp was in a lovely forest. I was glad to go upstream to a hidden spot and have a dip. As we ate around a campfire, we toasted the leader as this was our farewell party. We had made friends with the Russians and were sad to see the trip end.

The next morning we were met at the railroad station in a small village. We found the whole town gathered in gala clothing, waiting to greet us. They congratulated the commander on his march across the Caucasus. I found out later that this was indeed the training ground for the battalion that was sent to Finland in World War II. It was not so far off. I was never able to find out how large the battalion was. They were always scattered: foot soldiers everywhere in disarray, making camp in hidden gullies, far from us. When they loaded the freight cars to take the horses back to Rostov, I counted at least two hundred horses and four carloads of men.

The cars of the Red Army battalions were dropped off at Rostov. Helen, the woman geologist, and I shared a compartment for the overnight trip to Moscow. I climbed onto the upper bunk, leaving the two women frantically trying to write a report of all the speeches given on the trip to Georgia. They had not been told that this was required of them until they boarded the train. They were searching their notes in an attempt to recall who had spoken, what, and where. Periodically Helen would pull on my blanket to wake me and ask if I could remember what "so-and-so" had said. With tongue-in-cheek I dredged up some of the bright remarks made by all of the speakers and then went back to sleep.

Two days later I was heading for the scientific session in Moscow when Helen spotted me from across the street. Hurrying over, she explained that she had just come from a meeting with some high-

Women loading barges, Ob' River, Russia, 1937. Geologists' train is at right

ranking army personnel and they had demanded a fuller account of what was said by the mayor of a town near the Black Sea. Could I help her out? I gave her some of the oft-repeated phrases in praise of Stalin and his reforms and she departed satisfied. She had forgotten that I had been ill and went ahead that day with the doctor. My belief that Helen was no ordinary Intourist guide was confirmed.

My last day in Moscow was spent packing for the excursion across Siberia to Lake Baikal. We traveled by special train in sleeping cars and had side trips south of the railroad to visit mines, factories, and cultural projects. The Russians boasted about the "biggest" factories, mines, and cultural projects in the world and continually pointed them out to us, proud of their accomplishments. A miner named Stakhanov had been decorated for introducing methods that doubled the workday production. At the end of each long day of geology and sightseeing, we would remark, "This has been a Stakhanovite day!" I believe the Russians were anxious to have the foreigners return to their countries and tell about the wonderful things they had seen.

Everywhere we visited the stations had signs of greeting for the visiting geologists. When we were being taken by bus from the train at Sverdlovsk, formerly Yekaterinsburg, to our hotel, we passed the house where the czar and his family had spent their last days. I was anxious to explore the town and take a closer look at the sloping, shingled roof where the family were allowed to sun themselves. Ah, no! We had to rest in the hotel. We had been up most of the night before reaching the main line and our sleeping cars.

The young woman assigned to me and I went to bed. Soon I felt the familiar bites of bedbugs and took to the floor in my sleeping bag. As I watched a line of cockroaches descend from a crack in the wall, I decided I had enough rest. I dressed, left my sleeping watchdog, and descended in the elevator. Dressed in my working clothes with a bandanna tied around my head, I walked the streets, unrecognized. I found the czar's home and then went into a grocery store, feeling liberated from the perpetual supervision. When I arrived back in the hotel lobby, I was met by the much-concerned OGPU and trip leaders. They were certain I must have been spying and I got a real "shake down" about how dangerous it was to go out alone. The next day I had a new watchdog and was more closely guarded.

There followed a three-day trip in a small ship, up the Yenisei River from Krasnogvardeysk almost to the Mongolian border. It was the last time the group was to be together. We had been scheduled to visit some mines near Lake Baikal, but were told that there was some trouble in the area. We didn't know what, of course. The party had to return to Moscow. Five of us Americans planned to go on to China and then back to the United States by boat. We were told that they weren't sure whether we could go on. So we boarded our train with the others, believing we would be sent back to Moscow. In the middle of the night we were awakened and told to get all our luggage. We were going east.

The train was packed with soldiers. I was given a berth in a compartment with two sets of three-tiered bunks, with a narrow lane between. I spent a restless night in a middle bunk. We were shunted back and forth at various stations to give way to lines of freight cars filled with armored vehicles, large guns, and huge boxes of equipment. All were heading east. Was there a war? Finally, the next morning, the five Americans, two Japanese, and a geologist from Jerusalem were transferred to a more comfortable sleeping car.

George Bain, from Amherst, Massachusetts, came to my compartment. I no longer had a companion; my watchdog had gone west with the others. He said that we would soon be going around the shores of Lake Baikal and he very much wanted photos of the lake. He gave me his camera, saying he had left the window in the lavatory open a few inches at the top. I had to be sure that I didn't have any telegraph poles in the view as it would be a dead giveaway that the pictures were illegal. The whole next day the train went fairly slowly around the south end of the lake. We were often held up by workmen, who were frantically trying to finish this stretch of the railroad, which was single-tracked and had to be doubled quickly. We had always been told that the Trans-Siberian Railroad was double-tracked, but this stretch was still unfinished. The lavatory was next to the compartment shared by the two Japanese, who probably became suspicious about my many trips there. When we finally were taken off the train in the middle of the night at Chita, I was thoroughly searched by the customs agents. My three rolls of film were carefully examined. I had been allowed to keep the film that I had taken before my camera "disappeared" in Georgia. George Bain had anticipated this and sat up all that night underdeveloping the rolls I had shot of Lake Baikal, substituting his film for mine. The films had to be developed in Russia before we left the country. Luckily, the customs officials could make nothing out of the Baikal rolls, as they were blurred. George could finish developing them later in the United States. We had thought that the Japanese geologists would be helpful to us when we reached their country, but they completely disappeared. And they must have pointed their fingers at me. While the others only went through cursory examinations, I was searched from head to toe.

The next morning, going east from Russia as we approached Mukden in China, we saw soldiers standing on both sides of the railroad about every 300 feet, facing away from the tracks. This worried us so we went to see the American ambassador in Mukden. He told us we could not possibly go to Peking, as planned, because the Japanese had already captured it. They had not declared war, but were simply taking over China. It was called the "Japanese incident." He said six Americans had just arrived in Mukden, after three weeks of a rather harrowing trip from Peking. We could not travel by night, as the bridges were being blown up by White Russians, who were trying to sabotage the Japanese. The one we had crossed just two days before had been dynamited.

On the next day, in the dining car *en route* south to Seoul, I was sitting alone when a well-dressed Japanese man approached and asked if he might sit with me. It turned out that he had been educated at the University of Chicago and was most interested in my travels in

Russia. On departing he gave me his card and said if I needed any help to get in touch with him in Tokyo. He belonged to the Japanese Intelligence Service.

When we came to Pusan to take the night ferry to Japan, the boat was crowded. Throngs of people were pressing their way aboard. George and the others from the congress group had obtained berths and disappeared. Florrie, a friend from Barnard College, and I finally gave up. We decided not to be "pushy Americans" and retired, exhausted, to a bench. Before the boat set sail, a white-clad ship's attendant approached us and said that he had a cabin we might have. We were ushered to a large stateroom behind the bridge. It was luxurious. I believe that my "intelligence" companion had engineered this. My photographer friend George and his wife passed a dreadful night in the stuffy hold. Because of blackouts, no one had been allowed to go on deck. There was fear of Russian bombers from Vladivostok. It was a relief to arrive on Japanese shores.

Fuji Stew

JAPAN WAS A sharp contrast to the Spartan life of Russia. The hotels were clean and the food delicious. The scenery was like a picture: forests and flowers in profusion. We had three weeks to sightsee. We spent some time visiting an active volcano, Mount Aso on Beppu Island. We also took a lovely inland passage trip to Osaka to reach Kyoto.

In Kyoto Florrie and I were shopping when George Bain rushed up and said to pack quickly. Two of his former Japanese students, who were teaching at Tokyo University, were going to accompany us up Mount Fuji. It was September and Fuji had been closed to everyone because of the situation with China. There was a strategic weather observatory on top. We were to start our climb on the forested side of the mountain, at 600 feet above sea level; the summit is over 12,000 feet high. We spent the night in a Japanese inn, our bedding consisting of mats on the floor with wooden headrests. The toilet discharged refuse into a courtyard by means of a wooden slide.

After a restless night, we started out at dawn in a pouring rain. Three saddle horses and a packhorse had been engaged for our party. One of the Japanese students was accompanied by his wife, a pretty, frail, young woman. The three American women were to ride the saddle horses, while the rest walked. Three porters loaded the packhorse and we were off in the pouring rain through a beautiful forest of pines. This side of the mountain was used by local climbers. The rest of the tourists and Japanese who made the yearly pilgrimage up Fuji started at an inn high on the open slopes on the opposite side from where we were. Their climb was much easier than ours on a trail with small rest places along the route where tea was served and raffia slippers could be purchased to protect their shoes from the ash and rocks. Today, I am told, there is a road to an even higher starting point.

There were no huts or resting places for us as we sloshed along the muddy trail. Soon it was obvious to me that the Japanese woman was not used to hiking and would slow us down. I offered her my horse, which she gladly accepted, and I climbed on foot with the men the rest of the way. Shortly after noon we came above tree line and found ourselves in brilliant sunshine, above the clouds that had soaked us all through the forest. A halt was called, and one of the porters unpacked our lunch, a ball of rice wrapped in red seaweed with a pickled peach in the center. Mineral water was produced for the foreigners and wine for the Japanese. I was beginning, as were the others, to feel the effects of altitude. We were at about 9,000 feet and exhausted.

After a short rest, we went forward, slowly, breathing with some discomfort. The sun was intense and our lips began to blister. At 10,000 feet, the trail became too rough for the horses. They had to be sent back with one of the porters. The other two porters shouldered our meager belongings and food and on we struggled for another thousand feet of steep climbing. Finally, we came to the trail that was on the usual route for pilgrims. The last rest house was ahead, a small hut made of cinder blocks cut from the volcanic rocks. The roof was made of tin and the small windows were sealed tight with cinder blocks. One of the porters removed the blocks from a window, climbed inside, and forced open the wooden door. By now it was seven in the evening and we were tired and hungry. There was a large sunken square in the center of the gloomy, damp interior. The porters found some charcoal and started a tiny blaze to heat some water. We sat around this pit, with our feet dangling inside, and rested, with blankets wrapped around us. This was to be our bedding for the night. Then we went outside to watch a glorious sunset. As the sun set, Fuji's triangular cone made a show on the sea of clouds below us.

At 11,000 we were feeling altitude sickness. The porters produced rice balls again and a can of "bully beef" for us foreigners. No one was interested. I decided that we needed to eat something hot so I took the rice balls, the meat, and a cake of chocolate and added some raisins that Florrie produced, then proceeded to warm this mixture over the coals. The mess that was produced was horrible! A few mouthfuls was enough. Years later, whenever I met Florrie or the Bains, they kidded me about my "Fuji stew." The Japanese and porters, however, thought it was delicious. They consumed the whole potful. Next morning, there was a gorgeous sunrise that lit the clouds below with rainbow colors. Again, we saw the shadow of Fuji, this time in the west, as the sun rose above the clouds.

George and I were the only ones able to set out for the summit. The thousand-foot climb turned out to be a grueling trip; breathing was torture. We were not really acclimated; our ascent had been too hasty. But we pushed ahead. Fortunately, the snows had been late this season and we had very little trouble getting through the few snowdrifts on the path. At last we were greeted by the red torii on the top, a gate with no door. There was a small shrine and shelter beyond on the rim of the volcano. The wide circle of the crater lay deep below us. It was not shallow like that of Mount Rainier. This one had been formed by steam on the edge of the crater. Though exhausted, George insisted on walking on the rim to the observatory buildings, which we could see in the distance. Here, we were met with consternation by some angry scientists. At last an English-speaking member was located who asked how had we got to the top. Visits were strictly forbidden, closed to all because of the incident (they never used the word "war"). This was a strategic place for weather observations. We should be arrested. Of course no one there had the power to do so. We departed, much chagrined at our rough reception.

The way back to the hut was easy. Part way down we met the two Japanese men from our party, who were ascending slowly. The wife had stayed behind. After a long rest, awaiting our two friends, we started down. George's wife was having great difficulty. As a result of polio, one of her legs was shorter than the other. She always limped and wore a raised shoe. This condition caused her to stumble on the steep trail as we went downhill. She couldn't negotiate the deep ash we were encountering.

At first George tried carrying her piggyback, but he soon tired. At one of the small rest huts the porters removed a section from the tin roof, fastened a rope to the front of the metal, and made a sled. George forged ahead with great leaps and bounds, pulling her behind him. She was doubled up, with a scarf tied across her face as protection from the ashes, which George threw on her in his strides down the steep ash slope. She was quite a sight when we finally reached the inn at the end of the trail. Our suitcases had been delivered there by train. We piled all of our ash-covered clothes and sorry-looking boots in a heap, leaving them to be disposed of by the Japanese. We dug out a change of clothes and were taken to a room to clean up.

Here we were treated to a bath in true Japanese style. The four of us foreigners, as guests, were ushered into a large room with small stools surrounding a fifteen-foot-wide "bathing pool," filled with steaming water. Foreigners were to bathe first. George retired at this point, in deference to us. A young man came in and motioned us to sit on the stools. He scrubbed us with soap and water from his bucket before allowing us to soak in the tub. The picture of Florrie, who was quite stocky, sitting on her stool, trying to wash herself and shoo away the Japanese attendant, still makes me chuckle. It seemed a ludicrous sight to us and we collapsed in gales of laughter. After being scrubbed, I attempted to soak in the tub but pulled myself out quickly. It was scalding hot.

To complete our stay we went on by train to Tokyo to enjoy the beauties of country trips and to visit some of the shrines. Finally we boarded our ship to cross the Pacific. We had been so burned by the sun on Mount Fuji that we all had black-looking, blistered lips. The ship's doctor assured us that he would make us presentable by the time we reached the Hawaiian Islands. We were shunned by all on board, who thought we had picked up some strange disease on our sojourn in Russia.

The three weeks we spent in Japan were a blissful change from the hardships of Russia, a return to a more refined culture. After a brief visit to Hawaii, we would be glad to return to the comforts of home.

PART III

A Change of Pace

George, Marland, Betty, and Kay Billings, Wellesley, 1946

Marriage and Motherhood

ETURNING HOME after the trip to Russia, I was approaching another turning point in my life. My housemate, who was also an instructor in the geology department at Wellesley College, was anxious to meet young faculty members from the neighboring universities in hopes of "catching her man." So we gave parties, inviting our students as well as geologists from Harvard and MIT. I had no intention of ever getting married again. The breakup with Jock had been too painful. My life was now my own, a circumstance I found simpler than coordinating careers. I was selfishly free. I enjoyed the teaching, which I was able to combine with geological research, especially work in New England. Then fate intervened.

I found myself attracted to Marland Billings, the young scientist who was becoming a leader in the field of New England geology. We had met at various meetings and conferred when I was mapping the Mount Cardigan region. I fell in love again. But the pull of my emotions was at war with my desire for independence. Perhaps I could combine marriage with a career, I thought. Marland proposed and after much agonizing, I accepted. We were quietly married that spring, 1938. It turned out that I was the one who had "trapped her man," not my housemate.

By the age of thirty-six Marland was a confirmed bachelor and must have been equally surprised by his decision. Years before, when he had taken a two-year teaching position at Bryn Mawr College, a member of the Harvard faculty had told him that if he went to Bryn Mawr for two years and did not marry a Bryn Mawr woman, he was doomed to be a bachelor for life. The two other bachelors from Harvard who went at the same time had come back with wives. A decade later, he too had been caught by a Bryn Mawrtyr.

Our first summer together was spent continuing Marland's work in the Mount Washington region. We had long days following the streams and ridges and fighting the heavy undergrowth and blackflies. Years later, Marland was awarded the Penrose Medal, the highest honor of the Geological Society of America, for his contributions to geological science in mapping New Hampshire. In his acceptance speech he wanted to lighten the tone by telling an anecdote about that summer. As Marland was to report, we had followed a brook all day on the western side of Mount Washington, reaching tree line in the late afternoon. In exhaustion, I stretched out, spread-eagle, on the matted dwarf spruce near tree line. As I looked down at the gnarled trunks below, I remarked, "Now, I know where all the bodies lost on the mountain can be found." Higher up, the mats of stunted trees were knee deep. We were able to push our way through, but our dog got stuck, so Marland had to carry him on his back as we pressed on to the high gulf-side trail, which we planned to follow back to the base. All this was included in his speech, which was to be published later.

To my horror, he abandoned the written text entirely. Instead, he told how, on a cold September day, we had left the Lakes of the Clouds Hut, where we were staying while working in that part of the mountains, and dropped down into Oakes Gulf, a south facing cirque. We had worked our way up a small stream, bushwhacking when necessary. As the day wore on we got hotter and hotter and discarded our heavy clothing. I had seen a small waterfall above us and told Marland that I would go ahead and take a bath. In his speech, Marland reported, "When I came upon Kay, sure enough, there she was taking an ice-cold shower!" So this is what he remembered when he looked back over our first summer.

In marrying I knew that I was the one who had to change focus. Marland already had an established career. Since I was thirty-six years old and time was slipping by, we decided to have a family before it was too late. Continuing my teaching career would be a conflict, so I handed in my resignation, closing the doors to Wellesley College forever. Perhaps my friend Mickey had been right when she said a woman's life was not complete unless she had children. If we were not married by thirty-five, she had said, we should have children out of wedlock. Mickey did exactly this, having a child in China with a married man while continuing to pursue her peripatetic career.

That fall I became pregnant. Everything seemed to go wrong. It was a difficult pregnancy and I had to spend several months in bed. Like my father did when I was a child, Marland came to read to me at night to calm my fears and assure my sleep. Delivery was painful and I had to remain in the hospital for three weeks, waiting for my muscles to mend. On returning home I was forced to continue the bedrest so we hired a nurse to care for me and for our baby, a husky son whom we named George.

The doctors advised against having another child. Since we did not want George to be an only child, spoiled and selfish, we decided to adopt a sister for him. A year later, when we heard of a possibility of adopting from an orphanage in Canada, we headed north.

Adoption was not common in the 1930s. In fact, it was socially unacceptable. I knew of only one other family that had dared to trespass on these social taboos. It was believed by many that an adopted child might turn out badly and disgrace the family. We were willing to take that risk. After all, there were skeletons in every family's closet. We would do our best with both children. We believed that tender, loving care and environment would triumph over heredity.

The children in the Canadian orphanage, all under a year of age, were well cared for. We were told that most were the children of fathers who had been on ships sunk by the Germans in World War II. Their mothers were unable to support them.

The younger babies were adorable. We could distinguish different physiological features, but not personality traits, so we asked to see the older infants. We were ushered into a room with about a dozen babies on their stomachs who were getting their exercise by kicking and eyeing the stuffed animals placed in front of them. Like a magnet, Marland and I were simultaneously attracted to a little girl of eight months. She looked like a perfect match for our son. Although she was weakened by a bout of whooping cough, we knew we could make her strong. We were sure she would blossom.

Adopting a child in Canada in those days could take two months. There was endless red tape: adoption documents, immigration papers, etc. We signed all the necessary forms and returned to Boston to wait. We had made a rash decision. Was it the right one? The wait was tortuous.

Two months later I took this ten-month-old infant in my arms. She smiled, delighting the head nurse, who said that this baby screamed when most of the nurses handled her. We returned home on the night train. At the border checkpoint an immigration officer came to our door to examine all our papers and the infant immigrant. He had to make sure we weren't smuggling in an alien. And so Betty came into our family. We never regretted our choice.

Years later, when we were traveling back from Phoenix, where Marland had been honored for his geological work, I sat next to a mother with a tiny baby. We engaged in conversation and she confessed to feeling insecure about returning from Mexico with her newly adopted infant. I was able to assuage her fears, telling her about my experience of adopting Betty and how successful it had been. This new mother was delighted and introduced me to three other mothers, who were also bringing babies back from Mexico. I answered their questions the best I could.

Life would never have been the same without Betty. As a small child she would meet some of our friends and say, "This is my little brother George [he was a year older]. He likes mice; I like horses." As the children grew older, I would always get a chuckle when people would say, "Betty is so like you and George is like his father. From which one of you does she inherit her musical talent?" I would reply that she certainly hadn't acquired it from either of us rock-hard geologists! If I was asked by some thoughtless person who our biological child was and who the adopted one, my reply would be, "They are both truly my children. One was born in pain; the other was chosen."

When Betty was ready to enter the Winsor School, there was only one vacancy in the third class for which she was applying and there were four other alumnae with daughters vying for this spot. One of my relatives said it would be hopeless for me to apply since Betty was adopted. Biological children would get preference. I was angry and disturbed by this prejudice and during the interview, I told the headmistress about Betty's origins. She expressed her own interest in the effect of environment over heredity. Betty was accepted.

When Betty was fourteen, the U.S. citizenship laws were changed so that adopted children born in other countries could become American citizens after two years rather than having to wait until they were twenty-one. Betty took a day off from school to go to the ceremony in downtown Boston. It was an impressive occasion. Those of us with underage children stood up in front while a judge gave a speech about the meaning of citizenship. The new citizens were sworn in and each was presented with a small American flag. On her return to school, Betty was a celebrity.

Nevertheless, some of my relatives never accepted her, which saddened both Marland and me. Betty was a threat to their inheritance, which was tied up in a long-standing family trust. At this time adopted children did not have legal rights as family members. My own family split apart on this issue. In time, through the efforts of a group of adoptive parents, adopted children became legitimate "issue" and equal under the law in Massachusetts.

The War Years

WITH OUR FAMILY in tow, we decided to live in Wellesley, a short commute to Cambridge for Marland and a good place to raise the children. We built a house with a large yard on three acres of land, plenty of room for children to play and space for them to grow.

Once my family was established, I planned to return to my profession as a geologist. But it was difficult. The war years were on us and it was hard to get adequate child care. There were no day-care centers as there are today. I was lucky just to find household help. On occasion, couples would live with us: the husband would work in the community and the wife would care for our family. Sometimes there were children. One woman, a widow from Oklahoma, wanted to give her two daughters a good education. She lived with us a whole year, grateful for the chance to have her oldest daughter graduate from Wellesley High School.

In the winters, I had access to the Harvard library and a desk in a space adjoining Marland's office to do my work. In 1940 the Boston Museum of Natural History needed a curator for their mineral collection. I was appointed associate in geology and found myself involved not only working with their mineral collection but also organizing geology exhibits and as lecturer to their Explorer's Club, a group of twelve- to eighteen-year-old boys who were interested in outdoor education. I helped by lecturing and showing slides of Africa and New England. Occasionally I would conduct a field trip to the suburbs.

For many summers when my children were young, my sister-in-law was delighted to come to my rescue. She would spend the summer with our children while her own were at the beach with their father (my older brother) and his second wife. Her kindness enabled me to do a full summer's fieldwork in New Hampshire.

During these summers I began to work on a geologic map of the Monadnock Quadrangle in New Hampshire. I spent three summers covering the area. But I needed a companion in the field. Marland didn't want me to work alone in a wooded region where no one would know where to find me if something unforeseen happened. I was lucky to find enthusiastic boys from the museum's Explorer's Club, who were delighted to have the experience.

My first summer of fieldwork in the Monadnock region went without incident. Our greatest hardship was negotiating the tangle of downed trees from the 1938 hurricane. World War II was on and there was a shortage of aluminum in the country. I had found a rather large deposit of an aluminum mineral called sillimanite on Gap Mountain, just south of Mount Monadnock in my mapping area. The state of New Hampshire wanted more information about this occurrence and asked me to make a detailed study. To do this, I needed help.

My husband and a mineralogist from the University of New Hampshire agreed to go with me and make a plane-table survey. We climbed to the top of the knoll where the sillimanite was located and set up our equipment with the help of my assistant. Soon we heard a bellowing in the open fields below. Cattle had the run of the whole fenced area around Gap Mountain, so we didn't pay much attention. The sound came closer. Suddenly, we saw an angry bull ripping up sod. The men grabbed the equipment and climbed on top of a large glacial boulder. I remembered a fallen birch tree on the way up the mountain, so I called my springer spaniel and dashed down, dragging the dog with me as I climbed the sloping trunk, hoping that the bull hadn't scented us. The men were screaming and cursing. When the noise had quieted down and the bellowing had stopped, I went back to see how they had fared. They were setting up the equipment again. The bull had given up and gone off. They had kept him at bay by jabbing the plane-table legs at his nose.

We had worked for about an hour when the bellowing began again. We could see the bull approaching and decided we'd better take off, pronto. We had a long section of forested woods to go through as we rushed down the steep slopes with the bull close behind. On the other side of the fenced area there was a house on the road where we had left our car. When we finally climbed the barbed wire, we were only a few yards ahead of our pursuer. The three women in the house came out. They had followed our escape from their upstairs window, fearful that the bull would come right on through the fence. They said he threw sod, trees, and brush aside as he followed in our tracks. Despite his nose ring, his sense of smell was very acute. Luckily, he was stymied.

That night we stayed in a small inn nearby and reported this confrontation to the police. At midnight an officer appeared to question us. He said that it was illegal to have an old bull loose. According to him, they were the most dangerous animals in New England, causing several deaths every year. Before beginning my work, I had

Kay's assistant measuring on Billings Fold, Mount Monadnock, New Hampshire, ca. 1941

received permission from the state and had written to the owners to tell them when I would be doing the mapping on their land. It turned out that the man who owned the cattle was shipping them illegally into Massachusetts at night. The animals, which had Bang's disease causing paralysis in humans, could not be sold, and should have been slaughtered. He was trading them on the black market, as beef was scarce in wartime. The police had not been able to arrest him before, but now they could. Nevertheless, we decided to put off the mapping until fall. The mother of the boy who chose to go with me had been concerned about the dangers we might encounter in the "wilds" of New Hampshire. I had assured her that it was nothing like Africa. No wild beasts would attack us. I never did know how she reacted to the tale her son must have told when he went home.

Because of the war, people had been notified to report any suspicious persons, especially those carrying or consulting maps. I don't know how many times we were reported. One Sunday we had been away from my car all day and when we returned, somewhat later than usual, we found the sheriff waiting for us. We had been reported as acting suspiciously around a dam site. The sheriff was chagrined to find that I was doing work for the state.

Near the town of Troy there was a colony of Finnish farmers whose understanding of English was poor. I had difficulty persuading them to let me go through their land. One woman had forbidden me to look at the rocks in her chicken yard. She had a ferocious-looking bloodhound, tethered to his doghouse, guarding the territory. As I approached the nearby outcrops, he snarled. I sent my helper up the road with my dog and sat down, pencil and paper in hand. Her dog began wagging his tail. Gradually I inched toward him as he sniffed, eventually putting his head in my lap. I then proceeded with my work. I am sure that the woman blamed me if any of her chickens disappeared.

The third summer of work mapping the Monadnock Quadrangle went very quickly. I had the help of an intelligent geology graduate student from Harvard University, Ursula Marvin, who wanted the field experience. Eventually she became a prominent geologist, a specialist in meteorites. Her work included two tours in the Antarctic. I often wondered if her time with me had inspired her career. She went on to work with methods unknown to me.

With the United States embroiled in the Second World War, I was asked to return to the Monadnock region to check the coarse, dike-like granites called pegmatites for beryllium. Beryllium, contained in a blue-green mineral, was very much needed in some strategic work. This seemed a crazy idea to me and a waste of energy. I couldn't see why this was important. Little did I know that this element had been found to be the best material for the linings of the furnaces producing the atomic bomb. So back I plodded, but after a month I was told to stop looking. They had found some other method for dealing with the high temperatures in the furnace linings. Because the war had cut off mica imports from India, I was asked to investigate any possible sources in the pegmatites in my area of study.

A chance to teach came my way during the war. The professor of geology at Tufts University had gone into the armed services and I was asked to help an elderly geologist teach his courses. From 1942 to 1944 we shared the instruction. I took the Saturday morning course and all the laboratory sections. The Saturdays were a challenge. The football squad had signed up thinking that a class taught by a woman would be a "snap" and that they could sleep when lantern slides were shown. Tufts had a wonderful collection of slides of geologically related subjects. I assigned the men (there were no women in this section) to seats and proceeded to rush through slides of places related to the subjects they were studying. I fired questions at individual students, calling on them by name. Before I knew it, they were all awake and on their toes. At the end of the semester, several of the boys came to apologize. They said they had no idea that geology could be so interesting. In the laboratory courses, I was able to capture their attention by producing maps from all sections of the country. They quickly became efficient, learning to interpret the geological features of a region. Several of the boys were going off to the war at mid-term. When I ran into one of them a few years later, he told me the map-reading course had been invaluable.

In 1943 I had acquired a small camp in Randolph, New Hampshire, in the White Mountains, as a place to go in hay fever season. Since George had developed asthma, this seemed a good idea for him, too. My sister-in-law was delighted to come with me. We packed up, and using our gas coupons, off we went.

During the war Marland had gone off to the South Pacific on a war assignment under the Office of Strategic Services. I never knew where he was or when he would return. Finally, the war was coming to an end. After more than a year, Marland arrived back, unannounced. He recalls that the first thing I said to him on his return was, "Oh, dear! I have used up all your gas ration coupons!" We had been able to get horsemeat in Berlin, New Hampshire, and I fed him a meal of "steak." Betty remarked on how tough it was. I never told them till later that it was horsemeat. They wouldn't have touched it.

That winter, back in Wellesley, we went to Marland's older brother's home for Thanksgiving. They somehow had managed to get cream, which we had not been able to obtain with our limited food ration books. When pie was served for dessert, with a generous helping of whipped cream on top, Betty stuck her nose in it and asked what the stuff was and whether she could eat the cardboard under the pie! Their cook was scandalized. Her crust bore no resemblance to the sticky mass produced in our kitchen.

Children Come First

WHEN I LOOK BACK upon the days when the children began school, I get dizzy. They were growing up and their needs had to be attended to. During these years I was the chauffeur, driving back and forth, to and from an endlessly changing series of schools and social functions. I felt as if I were operating a carousel with children going round and round.

Nursery school was a gentle introduction to the increasing demand on my time. The school was nearby and both children could attend the same class. The similarity stopped there. George was quiet and well behaved; Betty was always into mischief. One day she hid in a chest of toys and couldn't be found. When the lid was lifted, her cover was blown. She spent the next morning in the fourth-grade classroom under the scrutiny of the headmistress. The punishment seemed quite severe for a four-year-old. When asked if she was ready to return to her own class, she replied, "No, I like it here."

Elementary school further differentiated between Betty and George. We were fortunate to be able to enroll both children in a small school run by Wellesley College under the auspices of the psychology department. We were told that Betty was bright, adaptable, and assertive; George, on the other hand, was retiring and would need remedial help for learning problems. The psychologist recommended that since George would need special schooling, Betty should have some privileges too. Sibling rivalry might be intensified by showing favoritism. Betty had horseback-riding and music lessons to balance George's private tutoring. We didn't want either child to feel inferior; we wanted both to feel equally indulged.

The Wellesley College early childhood elementary school ended in the third grade. When it became evident that the children's learning styles were different, it was increasingly clear that their personality development would be distinctive as well. Regardless, we enrolled them in the same school for their remaining elementary school grades. The teachers there encouraged the children to pursue their own interests and to develop their own abilities. Betty discovered a talent for music and mischief; George was still withdrawn. When Betty and George chose different secondary schools, the demands on a mother also doubled. Fortunately, carpooling compensated to some degree. But many days, I drove in endless circles.

George and Betty on Pine Mountain, Mahoosuc Range in background, ca. 1950

In time that driving turned westward. When the children were teenagers we decided to expand their education by taking them on a trip across the United States. We wanted to give them a feeling of the size and splendor of the country.

So we headed west. In those days there was no air conditioning in cars and we suffered the heat of the long days. We stopped at motels *en route* until we reached the Rockies, where we planned to camp out. Our station wagon was loaded with camping equipment, including two tepee tents, the same kind I used in Wyoming years before. Each night we would pick a likely spot and set up our site. Sometimes the children rebelled and toward evening would point out likely motels where we might stop.

In the Black Hills Betty became ill from food poisoning. We laid out her bedroll in the back of the station wagon across all the gear. Stretched out on the top of the heap she traveled fairly comfortably. We spent two weeks at a ranch in the Beartooth Mountains so the children could savor the western way of life. We also enjoyed horseback trips with friends who had brought their two girls along. Betty seemed to recover in the cool air.

The next part of the route was based on the localities where Marland had students doing theses. We camped with one of them in

Yellowstone Park and with another in the Gore Range in Colorado. After Denver Betty was ailing again, but she revived when we reached places where she could drink plenty of water. She had become dehydrated and thrived on those sticky milk shakes they make in the West. She continued to lie out on the mattress in back of the car.

At the base of Mount Whitney in California, we made camp. While Marland took off with a student who was doing a thesis on Death Valley, I spent two days with a group climbing Mount Whitney. We had horses and camped out in the open below the steep crags of the summit, 14,418 feet, the highest point in the western part of the United States. The ridge was knifesharp so I walked that part of the trip, not trusting the horse, who seemed to ignore the vertical drops on both sides. The air was clear and we had views extending east over Death Valley. Jagged peaks rose in every other direction. On the return I walked down the steep slopes until we were back in the forested area. During my climb the children rested in camp. They were happy not to be on the road again.

We continued on, up the Oregon coast, across the Cascades to Duluth. Here we loaded the car onto the ferry to cruise through Lake Superior and the "Sault" locks to Sault Ste. Marie on the eastern shore of Lake Michigan. Then we journeyed home via Canada and New York State. That fall, Betty wrote a long paper and called it "Seeing the West by Air Mattress."

Blackflies and Bushwhacking

I T W A S 1 9 5 2. A half century had passed. My life was settling down to a routine. Marland had decided that the Gorham Quadrangle in New Hampshire, north of the Mount Washington Quadrangle, should be tackled. This was to be a joint effort: we would work together some of the time and other times independently, he with his secretary, students, or assistants, and I with whatever helpmate I could find. I had a few friends with the exploring instinct who would go with me for a few days. Sometimes, I had to work alone.

To map the Gorham Quadrangle we camped out in the shelters on the Mahoosuc Mountains. We followed all the streams, did traverses across the ridges, bushwhacked where there were no trails, and of course, battled the blackflies and mosquitoes. The work was strenuous and challenging. We completed more detailed studies than we had in earlier years using the knowledge accumulated since we had worked in the adjacent Mount Washington region. Winters we studied the rocks we had collected and made detailed maps.

Throughout our excursions we were lucky not to have accidents or become benighted. One summer, while working in the remote mountains east of Berlin, New Hampshire, my friend Merle Whitcomb visited. She loved to explore and made an ideal assistant. Her one failing was to insist we go a little longer, a little further. One day we followed a long brook and by three o'clock had not reached the turning point. She insisted that we continue, hoping to reach the Appalachian Trail on the crest and have a path to swing back and down to the road where we had left our car. We bushwhacked through thick undergrowth and reached the head of the stream. Still no trail, just an impenetrable mass of "blowdown" from high winds and winter storms. We pushed our way in zigzags, back and forth. Sometimes we dropped a hundred feet on either side of the ridge. Carefully we checked our altitude by barometer, in case we misjudged where we were. After a rest Merle disappeared among the blowdowns to the solid ground below. She called and held her hand high for me to see. She had found a sewing kit. We were on top of the trail! But still it had not been cleared. In fact, this section had been closed for several years.

By then it was after five o'clock and we had miles to go. I thought I recognized some cliffs that I had studied the previous summer, when the trail was clear. Dropping down to avoid the blowdown of the ridge, we took a compass bearing toward the cliffs. There, we finally found the trail, close to the junction from which we could descend to the road on the north. The going was slow, as this trail had not been cleared either. It was dusk when we reached the junction. We had to make a decision. Should we sit it out for the night or try to work our way down by dark? We chose the latter course. As it grew darker, we took turns leading. One at a time, we felt for the trail or touched blazes on the trees. Then we called to the one behind to come forward. The moon came up, which helped us follow the course. At ten o'clock we reached the road and hurried back the two miles to our car.

By the time we reached Randolph, where a friend was staying with my children, it was close to midnight. Because Marland was away in Vermont with students, she was starting to organize a search party. She always insisted that we tell her where we were going and when we would return. We had told her never to send out for help until the following noon. If we got lost, we would sit it out for the night and then return home by daylight. She had been too hasty. We pointed to the map and asked her where she planned to send the search party. Since we had changed our course because of the blowdown, they would not have looked for us where we were. After that, we refused to tell her where we were going. We didn't want her to organize a useless effort.

I had another friend, Margery Hurd, who begged to go mapping with me. Margery was staying with her mother at the Shelburne Inn a few miles away. One morning, when I had no one else to accompany me, I stopped to pick her up. I planned to follow a brook on the south side of the valley and hoped it would not be too rough going. It was a hot day in August, but there were no blackflies. The lower part of the brook was steep and fairly open. It had unexpected long stretches of outcrop, so I was kept busy writing notes and taking measurements to record on our geological map. Margery disappeared ahead. As I rounded a bend, there she was, bouncing up the brook stark naked, her dungarees and sneakers thrown across one shoulder and blue nylon panties over her shirt on the other. Lunchtime came and we sat below a small cascade. Margery left her clothes beside me and took several delightful slides down the small waterfall into a large "pothole" below. Her bottom came out all green from the moss. I joined her for a quick dip before we had to go on. She was chagrined when we had to leave the brook and go into the brush. I believe she thought all my trips were frolics!

Because we made so much noise, we rarely saw animals on our mapping expeditions. Occasionally we caught a glimpse of a deer, sometimes a bear. Camped out one night in a shelter in the Mahoosuc Range, we waked to the sound of gnawing. We turned on the flashlight to find a large snowshoe rabbit sharpening his teeth on the log at the base of the shelter.

Blackflies were our most hated enemies. We had to wear heavy clothing to protect ourselves from their vicious bites. We found them in all seasons, in damp mossy places they had supposedly left long before. Concoctions to prevent their swarming around us were useless as we pushed through the undergrowth. Hornets were another hazard and I was prone to stepping on the entrances to their nests. I would often have my dog along who frequently ran into the pests and suffered the consequences. He also never learned to avoid porcupines. I always carried tweezers. When he came whining, I would thrust my hammer handle between his jaws and quickly remove the painful quills.

Nature's Watchdog

A s t h e c h i l d r e n grew older, I spent an increasing amount of time supervising their activities and studies. In the winter I would become housebound. Luckily, I found some household help, which enabled me to continue to spend part of each day doing research. I also became involved in conservation causes and activities, which eventually became an important part of my life's work.

My conservation work began in my own backyard. In the 1950s the town of Wellesley was undergoing a growth spurt, with developers planning housing projects in many of the available open areas. Contractors needed gravel to build the new roads wide enough to satisfy the new building codes and sewage lines had to lie in sands soft enough to remove later if breaks occurred. In time the sands of the Wellesley gravel terraces, located in the town forests and in the town-owned land near the water supply, became tempting resources. Wells were sunk in these gravels and truckloads of sands were removed from Morses' Pond Town Park, endangering the town's water supply. I was horrified. When I voiced my concern to the Public Works Department, they just shrugged their shoulders.

The trucks kept coming and carting away the gravels. Miles of trenches were dug for utility lines for the new houses, filled with the precious sands and gravel. I spent days following contractors' trucks and getting their license numbers in order to prove the thievery to the head of public works. I even took pictures to show him. But it was too late. The damage was done.

Not long after the gravel skirmish, the town engineers decided that the lovely, winding Fuller Brook, located in a small park in the western part of town, should be contained to prevent flooding. Some residents had complained that their cellars were wet when the brook spilled over its banks, so it was decided to build a cement-lined trench to contain it. The trenching had already started by the time a group of citizens banded together to fight. This movement later formed the core of the town's watchdog group, the Conservation Council.

The blocks used to contain the brook were set in gravel brought in truckloads by contractors. I wondered where the gravel was coming from. Following the tracks, I discovered that the contractors were removing gravel from the esker in the town forest, a narrow glacial ridge that had been the bed of an underground stream when the ice sheet lay over Wellesley. I immediately went to the head of public works. This time he had the "rape" stopped. The Wellesley esker was an extension of the large one in the Auburndale section of nearby Newton, which had been entirely removed to use as fill in downtown Boston. In Wellesley it remains a lovely ridge in the town forest, of much interest and enjoyment to the hikers and students who visit the area.

Our geological knowledge was suddenly in demand in the group's effort to help save Fuller Brook. We fought long and hard. Once again I took photos to show the selectmen and we invited experts to talk to town meeting members to try to convince them of the folly of tampering with the brook. Again, we were too late.

While the Fuller Brook destruction was in progress, for several days I sat on a large glacial boulder of coarse conglomerate along the path. When the bulldozers approached to clear the rock from their path, they found me guarding it and had to go around. For many years the boulder stood there, intact. Today the brook is a straight stream in a park flowing between unsightly blocks of cement, which have toppled here and there, just as we predicted. The cellars are still wet in rainy seasons and the ducks and birds no longer have their nesting places. And no one prevented the team of new and bigger machines, which came to make repairs on the collapsing blocks that lined the brook, from destroying the boulder. They broke it in two, so they could get by. To my horror, it is now twins.

Throughout my years in Wellesley there were always demands to run field trips of the interesting features left by the ice sheet. I took scout troops on tours, gave talks to school science classes, and led groups of bird lovers and others. Eventually a friend persuaded me to write a pamphlet on the geology of Wellesley so that the public and schoolchildren could learn about their land. It was first published in 1961 and has gone through five revised printings. Though written for lay persons, copies were ordered by universities across the United States, Canada, Europe, and Asia, and it was used as a text at the Wellesley Middle School. In the booklet, numbers were assigned to each locality of interest and entered on a map of the town. Afterward, when one of these landmarks was eyed by developers, we could say, "You can't destroy that. It is listed in the 'Geology of Wellesley booklet.'"

As Marland approached retirement, we knew we had to make changes. The children had graduated from college and were starting out on their own. Betty had married and was teaching French. George was becoming interested in mountain-climbing activities. We decided to move to New Hampshire since we no longer needed the large house in Wellesley where we had lived for thirty years. When the house was sold, we moved to a small cottage at the beach in Little Boar's Head, New Hampshire, where I was born. Marland was still teaching part time, spending a portion of his week in Cambridge. My conservation activities continued. Although it was too late for me to start a large project with the strenuous fieldwork involved, I soon found myself a new cause.

For years the Appalachian Mountain Club had run nature walks. I myself had conducted several geology trips. The organization planned a natural history trip to the Isles of Shoals, a group of nine small islands ten miles off the coast, situated partly in New Hampshire and partly in Maine. I was asked to go along and explain the rocks. Obviously, I had to study them first. Explaining geology is not like identifying the birds or the flowers of the area. For two summers I made several trips to the islands to survey the shores. Since no one had ever done this before, people became fascinated with this small area that offered an ideal place to study coastline rocks devoid of vegetation. The pamphlet I wrote as a result of my study remains much in demand today and has been reprinted many times by the New Hampshire Economic and Development Commission.

To explore the various islands I was able to find a young man who had a motorboat to drop me at various points while I mapped. He always came back to pick me up at five o'clock on the dot. The biggest problem I encountered during these visits was on Duck Island, which was used by the air force as a bombing target and was therefore "off limits." Early one morning my boat man landed me for a hasty visit while he watched the sky for planes. Suddenly, the lobstermen, who were pulling in their traps, sped off in their boats. I rushed back, after only a brief glance at the geology. We pulled away just as the first bombs fell on their targets.

There were other hazards as well. On Duck Island mud nests were everywhere, covering most of the rocks. The sea gulls nested on Appledore Island and "bombed" me when I got close to their hatchings. Though less dangerous than the army planes' bombs, they were still rather nasty. Appledore's other problem was the poison ivy, which was shoulder-high in many strategic spots. On Smuttynose Island was ragweed, everywhere. I was miserable. Except for the difficulty in getting up on the runway, White Island, with its lighthouse, was one of the most pleasant to map.

While we were living at the beach a friend, Annette Cottrell, appeared. She was in the vanguard of the conservation movement in New Hampshire and she had a new target. There was a large point of land near Portsmouth Harbor, Odiorne Point, that had been taken over in World War II by the government as a strategic fortification for Portsmouth, our East Coast submarine base. Since its bunkers and gun emplacements were no longer needed, the state was selling the land to a developer, who was planning to put up eighty or ninety houses there. With great foresight, Annette saw the area as the perfect place for a science center. She felt it should be preserved, the last spot on New Hampshire's short, eighteen-mile coast that had not been developed. To persuade the state of its possible use as a state park, she dreamed up the idea of having various scientists write a booklet, with chapters on the history, bird life, flora and fauna, and marine life of the shores. She wanted a chapter on the geology and asked us to make a study to include in this volume. Marland and I made as quick an assessment as possible and I wrote the geology chapter for the book.

The volume proved instrumental in saving Odiorne Point from development. Today, this area is an important teaching tool for the region's schools. University of New Hampshire students now have field trips to study the geology and to make more detailed studies for their work. It is a place for picnickers and nature lovers as well. Nearly 100,000 people visit annually. In recent years a science museum was added. Odiorne Point has become so much in demand that it is now open all year.

On my own I also undertook another cause, preserving the beach marshes. New Hampshire's tidal marshes along the seacoast give charm to a fast-growing region. In the early sixties these marshes were being threatened by developers, who were filling them in and building. The marshes are crucial to the food chain of ocean fish. Before the wetland laws were passed, rumor had it that someone thought the marshes at Little Boar's Head could be filled and used as an airstrip. The marshes were endangered and there was no organization in New Hampshire at this time to preserve them. I searched and found a conservation group in New Jersey that was involved in saving the marshes along their coast. Since there was no group in New England that could do this, I approached them to see if they would include our acres in their preservation efforts. They agreed to add our marshes to their growing collection of parcels to be preserved as a wildlife sanctuary in perpetuity. I donated the seventeen acres I owned and several others I was able to buy as a start. Then I persuaded other owners to donate the land they had inherited from their forefathers, who had used the marsh hay for their horses. Gone were the days when we saw round stacks of hay cut in the summer, scattered about waiting to be hauled on sleds to the barns when the ground was frozen. As time went on, more acres were added until all of the marsh was preserved.

Despite this success, my marsh work was not finished. I discovered that a developer was putting in buildings along the edge of the marsh sanctuary, filling in the wetland right up to the river's edge and narrowing its floodway. I was sure this was illegal. When I looked up his "building and fill permit," I discovered that he was required to leave a "buffer zone" twenty feet wide along the side of the river. A group of concerned citizens went with me to the state capital in Concord. I took along photographs. We were given a hearing before the appropriate committee and the attorney general ordered the developer to remove the fill and imposed a fine for every day he delayed. The illegal fill is there to this day. There was no agency and no money to enforce the order.

Finally it was time for us to decide where to build our retirement home. We wanted to leave the beach, which was becoming crowded, and settle in the White Mountains of New Hampshire, where we had spent so many years mapping the geology. We looked around and found four acres in Bartlett near North Conway that had a glorious view of Mount Washington. We built a small house that was easy to care for and close to the hospital and stores. Here, we could snowshoe and ski in the winter and hike the trails in the summer.

Despite the move, we found our lives continuing on as before. Although he no longer taught classes, Marland still had research papers to finish and areas to visit where more study was required. We

Marland and Kay mapping, Pine Mountain, New Hampshire, ca. 1968

made new friends who liked to hike with us and shared our interest in conservation. And here, again, we were to become the watchdogs of the environment.

Developers had already preceded us into this part of New Hampshire and they were gobbling up the land. We had chosen the area for its natural beauty and were determined to preserve it. We had a new challenge.

The Saco River, the dominant feature of the Mount Washington valley, bisects the villages of North Conway and Bartlett. The low Green Hills lie to the east, the higher Moat Mountains to the west, the Presidentials loom up in the north. The Saco has extensive floodplains, where farming had sprung up in the early days. It rises at the height of the land in Crawford Notch and is fed by waters coming off Mount Washington to the north and streams from the mountains on the south side. The river is the delight of campers and canoers as it winds its way to the Atlantic. Private developers wanted to control the floods and channel the river so they could use the floodplains for construction.

Marland and I had followed up the streams that poured into the Saco, studying their course as they shaped the land. The streambeds were being narrowed with dams, dikes, and fill to protect the abutters. This development sped up the flow of water in the channel and endangered the people downstream. We took many pictures to illustrate these infringements, wanting to educate the public about the hazards of interfering with the natural flow of the river. Our efforts were directed toward having the zoning laws enforced. The natives did not understand the damage they were causing by filling in the floodplains. They felt they had every right to do what they wanted with their own land. The zoning laws that had been enacted to protect the environment were not being enforced by the selectmen.

One particular stretch of the river caught our attention. An outsider had bought twenty acres of floodplain with a partially dry old channel which he claimed was "dry" land. He began to remove gravels from this channel and used them to build up the floodplain while selling truckloads of the gravel to developers for their new roads. To our horror he was building a dam to the island between his land and the main channel, which had shifted its course a few years before. The old channel was crucial in times of flood. The people across the river were having their banks eroded much more quickly because the old channel was blocked by his dam. The developer had also narrowed the floodway by filling the floodplain.

We approached the selectmen and talked with the Army Corps of Engineers, pointing out the damage that was occurring. The selectmen just sat back and listened. At least the engineers did not allow the dam to be built above the height of the normal flow of the river. Despite all our efforts, the owner built up the land and constructed houses on the gravel terrace, which was the result of digging in the stream channel. He made a road on the filled floodplain, which acts as a dike to protect his houses. He also built two large ponds, to raise fish, he said. These were below the groundwater table and provided him with more gravel and fill. It was frustrating for us to watch this destruction of the floodway.

In recent years a group of young people have banded together to try to have the new and tougher zoning laws enforced. They have even taken the selectmen to court for not enforcing them. I wish that they had been around in the days when we tried so hard to prevent the damage to the floodplain and the river.

After a few years of enjoying the peace and quiet of our new home in Bartlett, we were awakened early one morning by the roar of a plane over our house. Startled, I raced outdoors to see why it was flying so low. What I saw was a towplane pulling a glider from a glider-port that had sprung up across the river from us in the middle of Bartlett. It was the beginning of a nightmare. The noise of the tow planes made life miserable for all who lived in the formerly peaceful and quiet valley. Conversations came to a stop when the planes passed overhead. Something had to be done. Hopeless, everyone said! But I wouldn't give up. Several of us banded together and hired a lawyer. We spent two years fighting the legal battle. In the mean-time, the gliderport grew in size and scope.

To make our case, our lawyer told me to talk to everyone I could to get evidence of the nuisance. The local people were angry. One young widow with a small baby said the planes frightened and wak-ened her child. A truck driver who had to make the trip to Boston every night, slept by day. Because of the noise he was developing a heart ailment, becoming upset and nervous from the lack of sleep. Fishermen lost their solitude. A busy heart surgeon from Miami who had come to the mountains for rest could no longer listen to the clas-sical music he loved. Housewives became stressed awaiting the next noisy impact.

In time the gliderport became busier and grew into a commercial operation. We had to go to court. We hired a company that recorded airplane noise to take sound tests to prove how noisy the planes were. These tests were crucial in fighting our case. I collected evi-dence from within a ten-mile radius of the airport. Finally, we were due in court. We had already given our deposition before the owner's lawyer. A few days before our court appearance their attorney offered to sell us the airport at an outrageous price. This was our only sure chance of doing away with the nuisance. I was able to get a loan from the bank and other people donated generously. I believe the glider-port people thought we would refuse the offer. They were wrong. Suddenly we were the owners of the sixty-two and a half acres of beautiful floodplain. It was all groomed and graded. But how could we dispose of it?

I soon found myself in the real estate business. I had a large bank loan to pay. First, I offered the land to the town to use for recre-ational or educational purposes. If they built a needed new school, they could get matching grants from the state. They turned it down. "Who wants more land? We are surrounded by national forest," they said, "all non-taxable." I refused offers from developers and those who wanted to use it for gravel resources. Finally, we sold it to a man who wanted to make a family campground. He was able to offer half of what we had paid, but this seemed the best way to save the area as open space. We imposed restrictions that would assure it would never become a menace to the valley. We were glad to take our losses. Today the former gliderport is one of the loveliest campsites in the area. It is so popular that some people engage their site three years in advance.

As a postscript, a few years ago a man wanted to put a heliport in Intervale, in the eastern part of Bartlett. He had bought the land and was applying for a permit. Hearings were held and they called on me to testify about the impact of the gliderport on the community. My testimony helped to defeat his application. No permit was granted.

My work in this part of New Hampshire was far from over once we had solved the gliderport nuisance. Across the river from Bartlett, North Conway is bounded on the west by state parks and the mountains of the national forest and to the east by a small range called the Green Hills. The Mount Cranmore Ski area is located at their northern end. The broad Saco River Valley lies between the ranges. The Green Hills had originally been set aside as "common land" to be used by the seventy-five early settlers for their wood supply. In the mid-nineteenth century, when they were in need of money, the town fathers had sold the land to a granite company. Since then, the region had been lumbered and left in a wild state. There were lovely views from the summits, providing an ideal place for me to explore when I could no longer master the rugged higher peaks of the Presidentials. I became possessed with the idea that these mountains should be saved from developers for future generations to enjoy.

I spent years trying to work out some way to save the land. The Conway Conservation Commission tried to prove that the sale of the area by the town fathers had been illegal, but courts upheld ownership by the granite company. Then I approached the Nature Conservancy to interest them in preserving the natural area on Peaked Mountain, where acres of mayflower and rare plants flourished. The Conservancy became convinced of the land's value and tried in vain to purchase the Green Hills, but the granite company refused to sell. Years went by and I still kept pushing to find some way to save the area. Finally, the granite people decided to sell the whole of the Green Hills, but at a price the Nature Conservancy could not consider. A developer stepped in. In desperation, the Nature Conservancy began to deal. They found that they could obtain all of the higher land, 2,800 acres, at a fair price. The funds, of course,

Photograph by Anna Stearns

Kay (standing) lecturing to friends on Peaked Mountain, Green Hills,
New Hampshire, 1967. Annette Cottrell is at right

would have to be raised from private donations. The Conservancy
could only loan money, which would have to be repaid later.

I had an urgent call from Boston asking me to talk to my friends
to see what funds might be available. I hate to ask my friends for
money. Hesitating, I approached a Randolph friend, Anna Stearns,
who had hiked so many times with me in these beautiful hills. By this
time she was bedridden, showing the first signs of Alzheimer's disease. To my utter amazement, she said she would buy the whole of
the Green Hills as a long-hoped-for memorial to her parents. The
Green Hills were saved. Now they would be green forever.

Anna Stearns lived just long enough to learn that her dream of a lasting memorial to her parents had been accomplished. She died in April 1990. I wanted to be sure my friend Anna would not be forgotten. It was her generosity that had saved the Green Hills. I found a place on the top of Black Cap Mountain, with views of the whole Mount Washington valley, where an inscription could be carved on a flat granite slab so that future generations will know that it was preserved by Anna Stearns as a memorial to her mother and father.

The Green Hills are now under the stewardship of the Nature Conservancy, with an active committee to develop trails for hikers and for nature study and to determine where motorized vehicles should be allowed. It is a place to escape from the pressures of life in a busy, demanding world, an island of refuge, where one can still enjoy peace and solitude. Its value as a natural area will be its greatest appeal in the future when so few such places will be left.

Jet-Age Travel

A S MARLAND'S schedule lightened, we began to have more time to travel. In all his years of teaching, he had never taken a sabbatical. So in 1965 and 1966 we took an extensive tour of parts of the Far East and Southeast Asia, staying abroad for eight months. Wherever we went we met fellow geologists, who were happy to show us their areas. Marland lectured on his work in New England at some of the universities we visited.

We started our journey in Japan, lingering two days in the lush, hilly country near Mount Fuji. I remembered seeing the mountain's shadow reflected on the clouds when I had climbed it on my last visit to Japan thirty years before. We enjoyed the green forests and sparkling blue lakes at the mountain's base. Then we took the bullet train to Tokyo, passing tiny villages hidden away in the country with strawhatted farmers threshing their rice. In Tokyo we visited several of the shrines that are scattered throughout the city. The focal point of each was a large, gold-encrusted Buddha. I was especially intrigued by the gardens whose carefully groomed plants and trees were dwarfed in size to fit the scale of the tiny plots of land. My favorite was one that featured a pond with stepping-stones, with walkways of white sand carefully raked.

Taiwan was a gem of an island. We found an opportunity to take a small plane to the east coast to a marble canyon, where a road was being carved. There, a group of engineers invited us to join them in surveying an area where sections of roadway had fallen into the chasm below. Bridges had to be constructed to traverse these dangerous spots. An advisor from the U.S. Parks Service wanted them to repaint a red torii or gateway that was situated high on the forested slope beside a waterfall. He thought that if it were green it would blend with the landscape. One of the engineers asked my opinion. I replied that if I were to take a picture of the canyon, the red torii would tell me I was in Taiwan.

At the end of the gorge we dined in a small inn, where all twenty guests sat in a circle around a large tray laden with exotic dishes. It rotated much like a lazy Susan. We chose what we wanted with chopsticks. Since I was awkward with these implements, my engineer friend assisted me. He "wiped" his own chopsticks in his mouth and deposited a shiny ball, a sheep's eye, on my plate. It reminded me of raw oysters. I demurred. Marland was also unsuccessful with the chopsticks. He was grudgingly given a spoon or "baby helper."

Our visit to Cambodia was well worth the red tape involved. Angkor Wat was spectacular. Excavated by French archaeologists, some of the ruins had been restored while others merged with the tropical forest. Many of the cone-like vestiges were covered with tree roots, which enveloped them like the tentacles of a giant octopus.

We traveled through Angkor Wat in a small "put-put," a bicycle construction powered by a small gasoline engine with two seats over the front wheel and a native driver behind. We were the envy of a busload of French tourists who whizzed past us *en route* from ruin to ruin while we were able to make our way in a more leisurely fashion. In the evening we were entertained by a group of native dancers clad in costumes resembling those of the sculptures on the walls of the temples.

In India we met with a group of geologists from the International Congress, which had convened there during the summer. We joined them on a visit to Darjeeling at the foot of the eastern Himalayas. Kangchenjunga rose majestically from the deep valley below our hotel, its snow-capped peaks still unexplored at this time. Our eyes never tired of studying its jagged outline. At sunrise one morning we were lucky to get a glimpse of Mount Everest from Tiger Hill, its snowy summit rising high above the mountain range of the western Himalayas. This was the highlight of our visit to India.

Following the series of scientific meetings in New Delhi, we continued on our own. I remember a ride atop an elephant near the "pink city" of Jaipur. As we climbed a hill to reach an old fort, a small boy followed behind carrying a basket to collect the droppings. These would be made into large, flat pancakes and stacked in conical piles to dry to be used for fuel.

One night we slept in a large, drafty hotel that had been a maharajah's palace, long stripped of its rich ornamentation and furnishings. A side trip took us to the Taj Mahal, whose graceful profile reflected in the long rectangular pool was an unforgettable sight. The rich temples, surrounded by well-cared-for gardens, contrasted sharply with the barren landscape throughout this part of India. The people lived in poverty in small hovels crowded together, a depressing sight to witness.

Ceylon, now Sri Lanka, was enchanting. The tea plantations were laid out in symmetrical rows, a sea of deep green stretched out over acres of tilled hillsides. Women with straw hats picked the most tender of leaves, throwing them into baskets strapped on their backs. It was with great reluctance that I left this lushness.

Throughout the trip I had to make adjustments to the jet age. I wished that there had been some way to slow down our pace. I would have loved to linger longer, to learn more about the people we met and the places where they lived. I longed for the days when I was on trek in West Africa, where I had been able to live with the people, walk in their hills, see their crops and vegetation, birds and animals. Now I captured only a fleeting glimpse of the countries as we sped through.

Down Under

Our travels in Australia were extensive. First, we visited Perth in the southwest, where we stayed with one of Marland's former students. We arrived just in time to see the spring flowers, so much more colorful and exotic than ours. Red kangaroo paws were the most memorable. Then we journeyed on to Melbourne and our introduction to opossums. They lived in the open rafters of the dining room where we were being entertained before Marland delivered a lecture. We had to move from table to table like the Mad Hatter in Alice in Wonderland to escape the "bombardment" of droppings. It was hilarious. Our hosts were quite embarrassed.

Next, we flew north to Alice Springs and Ayers Rock. Our small plane skimmed just a few feet above the rock, and on landing, we got out to explore sandstone caves containing aboriginal drawings. Ayers Rock was not yet a tourist attraction. It was a wonder to behold as it rose from the endless flat plains, the monotony broken by a few giant monoliths.

We also visited the Snowy Mountains west of Sydney to see a new irrigation project that was so critical to the economy. They were tapping the headwaters of the rivers and pumping the water to the dry desert to the west. It was an enormous undertaking. We were housed in small cottages that had been built for Queen Elizabeth and Prince Phillip. I slept in her bed in two of our overnight stays.

In northern Australia, at Mount Isa's mine, Marland was taken underground; women were not allowed. I was given a surface excursion instead. We walked across a parched desert-like terrain in excruciating heat with temperatures in excess of 100°F. I imitated the kangaroos, who sheltered behind the shadows of the tall gum trees. They lined themselves up in the few inches of shade, their bodies to the front and their tails in line with the shadow. At a place along a dry river bed, there were fossils to collect. I quickly dropped one that was so hot it scorched my hand.

We spent the final leg of our sabbatical year in New Zealand. We viewed volcanoes and geysers in the North Island and at Mount Cook, on the South Island, we were taken in a small three-seater plane up the Tasman Glacier. When the clouds came in, we returned around the west side of the mountain, flying close enough to study the folds in the rocks. It was on the South Island that I found the one place in the world where I would be content to settle. With its alps and fjords, glaciers and beaches, and placid sheep grazing in lush fields, it seemed to me Christchurch would be a lovely place to live. It was very English, with beautiful gardens, a university town where the people were most cordial. In the center of town stands the statue of the famous explorer, Captain Robert Falcon Scott, a symbol of courage and endurance. The last survivor of the heroic trip to the South Pole, Scott died within reach of his home base. Too bad he never again saw this lovely city.

Machu Picchu as seen from near top of Huayna Picchu, 1970

Vertigo on Huayna Picchu

OLLOWING OUR RETURN from the sabbatical sojourn
Marland postponed his retirement for four years and continued teaching part time. He remained busy with seminars and
visiting students who were doing theses. He was also mapping in
New Hampshire. Since we could no longer take on strenuous field
projects, we were finding more time to travel. We visited Iceland to
learn about the recent lava flows from active volcanoes, then to
Europe, Scandinavia, the Caribbean. We wanted to see as many parts
of the world as possible in a lifetime. South America called.

There were to be a few weeks' break in January 1970 when
Marland did not have to teach. Our itinerary was to fly down the west
coast of South America, making several stops along the way. In Peru
we detoured to visit the Incan ruins high in the Andes. Of course we
had to visit Machu Picchu, the gem of them all. A train trip from
Cuzco brought us to the site high on the side of a river gorge.
Towering above the ruins rises the steep triangular cone of Huayna
Picchu. We decided to climb. Catching up with a tall Englishman
who preceded us, we followed him on the steep trail. The footholds
were hard to follow. The steps the Incas had cut were eroded. As the
cone of the peak steepened, we chose the wrong route. We searched
in vain for a safer way. The clouds swirled around us. For the first
time in my life I experienced vertigo. I felt as if I was sailing into
space, dropping a thousand feet to the river below. There were no
handholds. I was not a rock climber. Gritting my teeth, I pushed on
up, reaching the top safely at last.

On the sharp peak were remains of a small temple, where we
found three Frenchmen. They were rock climbers and had ropes
across their shoulders. They moved over to a sharp pinnacle to give
us room to rest. I didn't have the courage to ask them to help me
down. Somehow we would make it. This time, the Englishman did
not miss the easier route. I was not so dizzy on the descent. I decided
that many of the Incan slaves who had carried loads to the top to
build the temple must have fallen to their doom and I was sure that
human sacrifices were pushed off the peak to appease the gods.

After this hair-raising adventure, we flew from Lima south to
Santiago, then on to Port Au Mont. Turning due west we crossed the
divide between Chile and Argentina, traveling by boat and car to the

beautiful lakes region of Argentina. At Bariloche, we flew to Buenos Aires, where we managed to get air transportation to see Iguaçu Falls. Although very different from Victoria Falls in Africa, Iguaçu Falls is equally spectacular as it tumbles in cascades over low cliffs into a wide river. Victoria Falls plummets into a deep, v-shaped canyon. Both are surrounded by lush tropical forests. Beautiful large blue butterflies fluttered above one of the pools at the base.

Finally we stopped briefly in Rio de Janeiro, a city alive with crowds and color. The great, round, granite Sugar Loaf peak dominates the view. We found the statue of Christ reaching toward the sky an inspiring sight. Clear blue waters and sandy beaches surrounded the city. I was tempted to brave the surf myself, but the undertow was too strong. Through the years I have retained a craving to go for a swim whenever I can. Perhaps it's because I was born at the shore.

Back to Africa

THAT SAME YEAR a student of Marland's was doing his thesis in Namibia (Southwest Africa) near the Angolan border. Marland was asked to check his work. The company employing the student owned a copper mine at Tsumeb in the north. They sent Marland a first-class ticket which we then exchanged for two economy class. Our plan was to go down the east coast of Africa and visit the game preserves, which had been established since the days I had gone up through Central Africa the hard way. We visited Victoria Falls, which remained as before. At Cape Town we took the cable car to the summit and were able to follow the trails to various points of interest. I wondered if the cable car had been finished on my first visit to Africa so many years ago fate would have chosen a different path for my life.

From Cape Town we flew north to the copper mine of Tsumeb, north of the capital of Windhoek, in what is now called Namibia. Again, we encountered a mine in which a woman geologist was forbidden to go underground. The barriers and superstitions had not been broken. I was fortunate, however, to be able to see a part of the world that had not been discovered by the modern-day tourist. It was a wild country. Exploration for mineral wealth was just beginning.

We flew in a small company plane over Ovamboland, a region set aside for the natives. No one could enter without special permission. We landed at a large airstrip on the Angolan border. Already the English were envisioning this as a strategic point for the war that was bound to come. We walked along the Kunene River to study the rocks and even crossed into Angola. Then we flew back over the unexplored wilderness of the Zebra and Giraffe Mountains, named for their striped and reticulated patterns. If I had been younger, I would have returned to study this rocky terrain. I was sure that the geology would reveal the reason for the peculiar patterns.

We returned to the Tsumeb mine and proceeded north by jeep with the student and his wife and son to visit his research area and to review some problems he had in his mapping. We drove around the great dried-up lake at the border of Angola, the Etosha Pan, which fills up only on rare occasions when the rains come. Then we traveled west over desert lands into Ovamboland, where windmills occur at long intervals. They are used to pump water into troughs to ensure the survival of the game. At one of the windmills, milling gemsbok, with their long curving horns, stood around an empty trough, a pathetic sight. The windmill had broken down.

On our trip we were able to stay at small outposts near places where Marland's student had problems to solve in his geological work. One day a herd of elephants saw us approaching and decided to charge. We hurriedly reversed our direction. On emerging at the checkpoint exit of the closed area we discovered that the student's wife and I had violated the strict regulations imposed on those allowed inside. No women were allowed to travel in shorts. Long skirts were required so the natives would not be introduced to customs of the "outside" world. We wondered how long they could remain isolated in this way.

Valley of the Ten Thousand Smokes

B RUCE REED, a former student of Marland's, was the head of
the Geological Survey of Alaska. He had been urging Marland
to visit. So in 1972 we continued our explorations and
embarked for the north. We would go first to the area where Bruce
was working, then travel north to see Mount McKinley and on to the
very northern tip of Alaska, Point Barrow.

Bruce met us at Anchorage and flew us in his "float plane" to his
homestead on Lake Iliamna, a large lake southwest of Anchorage.
As we flew along the Cook Inlet, we searched for an opening in the
clouds that covered the range to the north of us. We finally found a
pass that took us below the snowy peaks in a zigzag course. Bruce
knew of my interest in glaciation and flew us on a side trip up several
of these glaciers. It was scary. I saw no place where a float plane could
land if we got in trouble. Iliamna Lake was a welcome sight.

Bruce had the use of a helicopter for a month so he could collect
samples in remote places for radiometric dating of the rocks. We
spent two days with him and a visiting geologist from California as
"excess baggage" while they visited key areas. The geologist's family
were also staying the summer at Lake Iliamna, where they had built
a cabin and were "homesteading." They were delighted to have company in this remote spot and glad to get the fresh supplies that Bruce
had packed.

The next day we flew to locations that Bruce had previously visited on foot. The pilot was able to place his skids down in the most
unlikely places, with just inches to spare from disaster. At lunch in a
remote area Bruce suddenly realized he should have reported his
position to his wife, Kitty, so that she would know where to send a
search party if we didn't return that night. I went back to the plane
with the pilot to radio the message. His end of the radio conversation went something like this: "Hi, no! How should I know where we
are? Bruce has all the maps and he is way over there. We are out here
somewhere. I don't think he even knows where we are. Well, so long."

That night after supper, Kitty said we were out of ice. "OK. Into
the plane, Cap. You people come along for the ride," said Bruce. So
in we piled, soaring up to the heights above the lake and landing on
a narrow ridge between two small glacial lakes that were partially
melted. Bruce and Cap grabbed two burlap bags and a hammer and

slid down, leaving us to admire the scenery. The alpine wild flowers were abundant, many kinds I had never seen. I quickly gathered as many samples as I could though they were loaded with hunks of ice from the lake. I knew Kitty was collecting flowers for someone at Berkeley, who was writing a book about the alpine flowers of Alaska. She would be delighted to find I had picked several that she had not seen before.

We then flew on to the dormant volcano, Mount Iliamna, and circled the tiny crater. Though it was night, there was still brilliant sunshine at this high altitude and Bruce insisted that Cap land in the soft snow at the base of the cone. He wanted us to have a photo of the mountain. The snow was very squishy; we were afraid we would sink. It was a quick stop.

The following day we flew west to Katmai National Park, passing over the McNeil River, where bears could be seen going down to the shore to catch salmon. We saw several of the huge brown bears headed for their favorite fishing spots. One female rose high on her haunches and "batted" her paws at the helicopter, thinking she was protecting her two cubs from a strange enemy. Then we flew close to Mount Katmai and landed on the flanks of Novarupta crater, which had spewed only a few years before. The previous year Bruce had brought the first astronauts to walk on the moon to this same place to see the fresh lava and ash that had not had time to show any signs of weathering. They were being prepared for what they would probably find on the moon's surface.

Suddenly Cap called out, "Quick! To the plane! A 'willy wally' (williwaw) is coming." The winds increased in ferocity. So down the Valley of the Ten Thousand Smokes we went, smothered in clouds of ash rising around us. The valley had "steamed" for many years and was covered with 100 feet of ash, thereby earning its name. We were glad to come out in sunshine to the fishing lodge on a small lake where Bruce left us. From here we were to head back to Anchorage and the remainder of our tour of Alaska.

The next day, before a plane came to take us back to Anchorage, we took a bus up the valley we had descended, to see the deep ash that had covered the river course in a previous eruption. When our guide found out we had flown down the valley the day before in the "willy wally," he said, "Oh! We heard that plane and hoped you would make it out safely. We no longer use helicopters here. We lost two in the past three years."

The Galápagos Sea Lion

THE YEARS WERE slipping by and we were growing old. It was 1980. Marland had fully retired and we were spending more than half the year in Bartlett. For the winter months we took a house in Wellesley so that we would be near relatives and friends, as well as the best medical facilities. We did not want to go into a retirement home as many of our older friends were doing.

One more trip tempted us, a visit to the Galápagos Islands with a group of geologists. Off we went to Quito, the capital of Ecuador, to Baltra, where there was a small air strip. Here, twelve of us boarded a small cruise ship to some of the Galápagos Islands. The fresh lava flows, volcanoes, and the flocks of exotic birds made it one of the most spectacular places we had visited.

On one excursion ashore I took a swim in a cave that was once the fiery tube of a lava flow, since flooded by the sea. When the surges of the tide caught me, I struggled to get back to the place where I had entered the tube. I didn't have flippers and had never used my snorkel under water, but I thought I had to swim under water to get out. Spying a baby seal high up on the side of the walled enclosure, I decided to climb up the cliff. If he could get up that wall, I could, too. The leader of our group had come in through the tube and saw where I was stuck. He coaxed me down, leading me out to safety. I was no longer the strong swimmer of my youth.

Female sea lions lay on the beach in great numbers and paid no attention to visitors. But the male, guarding his harem from the water, would become belligerent if he thought there was a threat. One male came after me when he saw me alone taking photos. He charged and chased, barking and baring his teeth. I ran in circles to escape, barely making the bank at the end of the beach's edge before he caught up with me. I was scared and glad to escape those fangs. Marland had been watching, but was unable to be of any help. He had difficulty walking in some of the rocky gorges and had fallen twice. Sadly, we began to realize that we could no longer keep up with the young. We would have to give up our geological explorations and our world travels. Now I would have to be content myself with memories. I could still read about the places I had visited and share my recollections with friends.

Golden Anniversary

INALLY, THE DAY approached when Marland and I had been married fifty years. It was 1988. We wanted no fanfare or celebrations. Instead, we decided to take our children and grandchildren to Bermuda so they would have memories of us still active and alert and enjoying life, not too old and crippled with age. Since the grandchildren's vacations did not coincide, we went twice. Our son George could not join us, but Betty was able to leave her job in Washington and come on our second trip. Unbeknownst to us, this was the last time we would have a visit with her. Only two short years later she was taken by a swift-moving cancer. She had been the life of the party, vivacious, witty, and full of fun. We realized how lucky we had been to have had this wonderful person as our daughter for so many years.

Bermuda had changed from the time I had visited my mother there sixty-five years earlier when I was a student at Columbia University. Automobiles were allowed; there were motorbikes everywhere. Hotels and tourists abounded. But Bermuda was still very English. White stucco houses were tucked in the hillsides. The Bermudans had saved the most beautiful stretch of coast on the south as a parkway for all to enjoy. The little coves with their pink and white sandy beaches, with crystal clear bluish-green water, could be reached by short trails. Caves and grottos lined with stalactites and stalagmites were fascinating to explore.

This trip was to be the end of our travels: old age infirmities were settling in. We were grateful that we had been active so long and that our minds still remained clear.

If the memory of us dims as the years go by, our grandson will never forget being dragged by a graceful dolphin across a flooded cave in a rowboat. And our granddaughter will be able to recall the thrill of exploring a dimly lighted cave through which flowed an underground river.

It was my ninetieth birthday and a new science center was to be dedicated at Odiorne Point State Park, New Hampshire. Since I had worked with Annette Cottrell so many years before, the schools in the region, and even distant ones, had found it an invaluable resource for teaching natural history. It has become a popular spot for tourists and for those who want open space. A second booklet was being prepared, containing all the natural history subjects in which Marland and I had shared. I would go to the dedication, but without Marland. He, too, was ninety years old. His legs and eyesight had failed. I would make a trip as a birthday present to myself, one more chance to smell the sea and hear the waves.

I drove myself past the house in Little Boar's Head where I was born. There were strangers inside. A breakwater had been built to protect the beach where I had played. Where the boardwalk had crossed the low dunes, there was now a parking lot, with meters. All spaces had been taken by eleven that morning. Everything had changed. I continued on over the "head," which the waves were eroding. Sugar Loaf, the large glacial boulder on Rocky Beach, was still there. I drove to the lovely state park at Wallis Sands, where I stopped and ate my picnic lunch and went wading in the cold sea water. The long sandy beach beyond beckoned me. To reach it, I had to climb over the breakwater, which was made of large angular rocks. My eyes misjudged my steps. I fell, and cut my leg. I looked longingly at the beach and sighed. It was time to stop. I had to face it. I was ninety years old! (Despite this mishap, I did make it to the dedication ceremony that evening, with bandaged leg.)

Laying Down My Pen

AND SO, Carol "the Curious," the voice from Wyoming. I have written this book to answer your questions. I began my story with my childhood at the dawn of the twentieth century. Then the many stepping-stones upon which my career was built. My schooling. The decisions I made. My thesis work in the Laramie Mountains when I had the world to conquer. Trapped in a forest fire. Prospecting for gold in West Africa and riding horseback in Stalin's Russia. Mapping and fighting blackflies in New Hampshire. Continuing my career while raising two children. My conservation work. A full life. Yes, I had finally earned the title of "'laidy' geologist," first given to me deep in the shaft of that Butte mine so many years ago.

At long last, as I lay down my pen, I look out at Mount Washington. I see the spot high up on the head wall of Oakes Gulf where there is a small waterfall. It was there that I enjoyed that ice-cold shower late that September afternoon so long ago. As darkness creeps across the mountain and the shadows lengthen, memories crowd in, and I say to myself, "Yes. It is growing dark, Gramma."

Kay at Lucy Brook, North Conway, New Hampshire, 1993

Photograph by George Billings

Curriculum Vitae of
Katharine Fowler-Billings

1902	Born June 12 at Little Boar's Head, N.H.
1902–1906	Winters at Newbury Street, Boston
1906–1923	Winters in Boston at One Plymouth Street
1913–1921	Student at Winsor School
1918	Father's death
1921–1925	Bryn Mawr College, B.A., 1925
1921	Camp counselor
1922	"Grand Tour" of Europe
1923	Athletic chaperone to three children
1924	Woods Hole invertebrate biology course
1925	Summer circling the western part of the U.S.
1926	University of Wisconsin, M.A.
	Summer: the Black Hills; Glacier National Park
1926–1929	Columbia University, Ph.D., 1930
1927	University of Wyoming field camp; thesis fieldwork
1928	Laramie Mountains thesis fieldwork
1928	Mother's death in Sicily
1929	Geological congress in Africa; Cape to Cairo trip
1929	December 14, married to "Jock" Lunn
1930	Winter trip to Saint Moritz
1930–1933	Sierra Leone, West Africa
1930–1931	Geological mapping of iron ore
1932–1933	Gold prospecting for mining company
1933	Trip to Gold Coast and Nigeria
1935–1938	Instructor in geology, Wellesley College
1935–1937	Geological mapping in the Cardigan Quadrangle, New Hampshire
1937	Geological congress in Russia: horseback trip across Caucasus; ascent of Mount Fuji
1938	April 23, married Marland P. Billings; mapping in Mount Washington Quadrangle
1939	Son George born
1940	Daughter Betty born
1941–1943	Mapping in Monadnock Quadrangle
1942–1943	Instructor in geology, Tufts University
1949–1953	Geological mapping in Gorham Quadrangle

1954	Western trip with children
1955–1956	Geological mapping in the Isles of Shoals Quadrangle
1960	Geological congress in Copenhagen; extensive travels in Europe
1965	Construction of retirement home in Bartlett, New Hampshire
1965–1966	Marland's sabbatical, extensive travels to Far East, including Taiwan, India, Australia, New Zealand
1970	Travel to South America, African game reserves, and Namibia
1972	Travel to Alaska
1980	Travel to Galápagos Islands
1988	Golden wedding anniversary trip to Bermuda
1992	Ninetieth birthday on New Hampshire coast

Publications

Fowler, Katharine Stevens, 1926. *Glacial drainage changes in northeastern United States* [M.A. thesis], Milwaukee, University of Wisconsin at Milwaukee

Fowler, Katharine Stevens, 1930. *The anorthosite area of the Laramie Mountains, Wyoming* [Ph.D. thesis], New York, Columbia University.

Fowler, Katharine Stevens, 1930. The anorthosite area of the Laramie Mountains, Wyoming. *American Journal of Science*, v. 19, pp. 305–315, 373–403.

Fowler-Lunn, Katharine, 1933. Hematite iron ores of Sierra Leone, West Africa. *Mining Journal* (London), v. 184, pp. 52–53.

Fowler-Lunn, Katharine, 1934. Molybdenite in Sierra Leone. *Mining Magazine*, v. 51, pp. 73–75.

Fowler-Lunn, Katharine Stevens and Kingsley, Louise, 1937. Geology of the Cardigan quadrangle, N.H. *Geological Society of America Bulletin*, v. 48, pp. 1363–1386.

Fowler-Lunn, Katharine S., 1938. *The Gold Missus: a woman prospector in Sierra Leone*. New York, Norton, 303 p.

Fowler-Billings, Katharine, 1941. Unfolding Mount Monadnock. *The New England Naturalist*, no. 12 (November), pp. 9–11.

Fowler-Billings, Katharine, 1942. Geological map of the Cardigan quadrangle, New Hampshire. *Geological Society of America Bulletin*, v. 53, p. 177.

Fowler-Billings, Katharine and Page, Lincoln R., 1942. *Geology of the Cardigan and Rumney quadrangles, New Hampshire*. New Hampshire State Planning and Development Commission Mineral Resource Survey, Concord, N.H., 31 p. with illustrations and map.

Fowler-Billings, Katharine, 1943. Mica hunting in New Hampshire. *Bryn Mawr Alumnae Bulletin*, v. 23, no. 3, pp. 1–4.

Fowler-Billings, Katharine, 1944. *Sillimanite deposits in the Monadnock quadrangle.* New Hampshire State Planning and Development Commission Mineral Resources Survey, part 8, Concord, N.H., 14 p. with illustrations and maps. Reprinted 1949.

Fowler-Billings, Katharine, 1944. Igneous and metasedimentary dikes of the Mount Washington area, New Hampshire. *Geological Society of America Bulletin,* v. 56, pp. 1255–1278.

Billings, Marland P., Fowler-Billings, Katharine, Chapman, Carleton A., Chapman, Randolph W., and Goldthwait, Richard P., 1946. *Geology of the Mount Washington quadrangle, New Hampshire.* New Hampshire State Planning and Development Commission. Concord, N.H., 56 p. with illustrations and map. Revised and reprinted 1979.

Billings, M.P., Chapman, C.A., Fowler-Billings, K., and Goldthwait, R.P., 1946. Geology of Mount Washington quadrangle, New Hampshire. *Geological Society of America Bulletin,* v. 57, pp. 261–274.

Fowler-Billings, Katharine, 1949. Geology of the Monadnock quadrangle, New Hampshire. *Geological Society of America Bulletin,* v. 60, pp. 1249–1280.

Fowler-Billings, Katharine, 1949. *Geology of the Monadnock quadrangle, New Hampshire.* New Hampshire State Planning and Development Commission, Concord, N.H., 43 p. with illustrations and map.

Fowler-Billings, Katharine, 1959. *Geology of the Isles of Shoals.* New Hampshire State Planning and Development Commission, Concord, N.H., 51 p.

Fowler-Billings, Katharine, 1961. *Geology of Wellesley.* Wellesley Conservation Council, Inc. Revised and reprinted, fifth edition, 1984, 42 p.

Billings, Marland P. and Billings, Katharine F., 1973. *Geology of the Odiorne Point area.* Odiorne Point State Park Natural Science and Historical Studies, Information Center, New Hampshire Department of Resources and Economic Development, Concord, N.H., pp. 1–7.

Billings, Marland P. and Fowler-Billings, Katharine, 1975. *Geology of the Gorham quadrangle, New Hampshire — Maine.* New Hampshire Department of Resources and Economic Development Bulletin no. 6, Concord, N.H., 120 p. with illustrations and map.

Billings, Marland P. and Billings, Katharine F., 1992. *The geological features of Odiorne Point: Exploring Odiorne Point. A guide to social and natural history.* Friends of the Odiorne Point, Inc., Rye, New Hampshire, pp. 37–49.

Billings, Katharine Fowler, 1992. The Long Road to Save the Green Hills of Conway, New Hampshire. *Appalachia,* v. 49, no. 1, pp. 54–59.

Transactions

The constitution of the Connecticut Academy of Arts and Sciences, founded in 1799, declares that "the object of this Academy is to cultivate every art and science which may tend to advance the interest of a free and virtuous people." Over the years it has been the goal of the Academy to represent the arts, humanities, and sciences in Connecticut through its meetings and publications. From 1810 to 1816, the Academy published 25 papers in the first volume of its new journal, *Memoirs*. In 1818, the Academy abandoned publication of *Memoirs* when Benjamin Silliman the elder inaugurated the new *American Journal of Science,* a more frequent and regular medium of publication. However, the Academy found that it had available a considerable amount of material in a number of fields which was not considered appropriate for publication in the *American Journal of Science.* Thus *Transactions,* a new series of publications, was inaugurated in 1866.

The third volume of the *Transactions* of the Connecticut Academy of Arts and Sciences gave the world the study by Josiah Willard Gibbs the younger "On the Equilibrium of Heterogeneous Substances," which provided the basis for physical chemistry. *Transactions* continue to be published at the rate of a volume or two every two or three years. *Memoirs* reappeared in 1910, this time in quarto form for major illustrated works.

SELECTED PUBLICATIONS OF INTEREST

MARGARET LEAVEY
Looking for the Armenians:
Eli Smith's Missionary Adventure, 1830–1831
1992   88 PP. $16.00   PAPER

ELIAS J. MARSH
The Sands of Yesteryear: Arabia Petraea
1994   102 PP. $16.00   PAPER

LEOPOLD POSPISIL
Obernberg: A Quantitative Analysis
of a Tirolean Peasant Economy
1995   420 PP. $59.50   CLOTH